D1707466

BELLE KEARNEY

A
SLAVEHOLDER'S
DAUGHTER

BY

BELLE KEARNEY

ELEVENTH EDITION

NEGRO UNIVERSITIES PRESS
NEW YORK

Originally published in 1900
by Abbey Press

Reprinted 1969 by
Negro Universities Press
A Division of Greenwood Publishing Corp.
New York

SBN 8371-2196-5

PRINTED IN UNITED STATES OF AMERICA

I wait for my story—the birds cannot sing it,
  Not one as he sits on the tree;
The bells cannot ring it, but long years, O bring it!
  Such as I wish it to be.

—JEAN INGELOW.

CONTENTS

A Slaveholder's Daughter

CHAPTER I

THE OLD SOUTH

A land without ruins is a land without memories;—a land without memories is a land without history. A land that wears a laurel crown may be fair to see; but twine a few sad cypress leaves around the brow of any land, and be that land barren and bleak, it becomes lovely in its consecrated coronet of sorrow, and it wins the sympathy of the heart and of history. Crowns of roses fade—crowns of thorns endure. Calvaries and crucifixions take the deepest hold on humanity. —ANON.

THE South was in its glory. It was very rich and very proud. Its wealth consisted of slaves and plantations. Its pride was masterful from a consciousness of power. The customs of society retained the color of older European civilization, although the affairs of state were conducted according to the ideals of a radical democracy. Its social structure was simple, homogeneous. Three castes existed. The slaveholders constituted the gentry. Generally, those of this class served in the legislatures, studied law, medicine, theology; con-

ducted extensive mercantile enterprises and controlled
their private finances,—seeking recreation in hunting,
traveling, entertaining, and in the cultivation of the
elegant pursuits that most pleased their particular turn
of mind.

The life of the great landowners and slaveholders
resembled that of the old feudal lords. The overseer
stood between the master and the slave in matters of
detail. He conducted the local business of the plantation, managed the negroes, and was the possessor of
almost unlimited power when the less serious-minded
planter preferred his pleasures to his duties. The middle class carried on the concerns of commerce and the
trades incident to a vast agricultural area, and were the
men of affairs in its churches and municipalities. The
third class constituted a yeomanry,—small farmers who,
for the most part, preempted homesteads on the poorer
lands, sometimes owning a few slaves, and who lived
in a world of their own,—the westward drift from the
Atlantic seaboard and the Blue Ridge mountains, with
an inherited tone of life that defied change until the
public school, of post-bellum origin, began its systematic inroads on the new generation.

Ladies of wealth and position were surrounded by refinements and luxury. They had their maids and coachmen and a retinue of other servants. There was a time-
honored social routine from which they seldom varied;
a decorous exchange of visits, elaborate dinings and
other interchanges of dignified courtesies. Every entertainment was punctilious, strongly suggestive of colonial gatherings. No young woman went out un-

chaperoned. Marriage was the ultimatum of her existence and was planned for from the cradle by interested relatives. When the holy estate had been entered, women glided gracefully into the position of the most honored occupant of the home and kept their trust faithfully, making devoted wives and worshipful mothers.

The popular delusion is that the ante-bellum Southern woman, like Christ's lilies, "toiled not." Though surrounded by the conditions for idleness she was not indolent after she became the head of her own household. Every woman sewed, often making her own dresses; the clothing of all the slaves on a plantation was cut and made by negro seamstresses under her direct supervision, even the heavy coats of the men; she ministered personally to them in cases of sickness, frequently maintaining a well managed hospital under her sole care. She was a most skillful housekeeper, though she did none of the work with her own hands, and her children grew up around her knees; however, the black "mammy" relieved her of the actual drudgery of child-worry.

The women of the South, in the main, realized their obligations and met them with reflective efficiency. Notwithstanding their apparent freedom from responsibility and their outward lightness of character, there was the deepest undertone of religious enthusiasm pervading their natures; and this saving grace has clung to the Southerners through all their changing fortunes. They are the most devout people in this nation to-day. Among them is found less infidelity,—fewer " isms "

have crept into their orthodoxy. As they have remained the most purely Anglo-Saxon, so have they
continued the most reverent. The army of governesses
and public school teachers was made up of gentle-
women of reduced means, the large middle class, and of
women from the North. Teaching, sewing and keeping boarders were about the only occupations open to
women of that day by which they could obtain a liveli-
hood.

Mississippi, like her sister states, was at the height
of prosperity. The wealthier classes were congregated
in the counties bordering on the great river, and its trib-
utaries, and in the rich prairie belt of the north-east
section. Madison was one of the leading counties.
Around the little village of Vernon, located in its south-
western portion, there stretched vast landed estates
owned by ten or twelve families. On each plantation
was an elegant residence for the master's household,
and a cluster of small cabins known as the "quarters"
where the negroes lived. On one of these plantations
my father established himself after his marriage. It
came to him with his slaves as an inheritance. The
majority of his neighbors were his relatives, the rest
were personal friends. These constituted a congenial
and delightful society. At the beginning of each summer the families migrated to the Gulf of Mexico, to the
mountains of Tennessee and Virginia, or to the Northern states and Canada. The ennui of the winter season was avoided by visits to New Orleans and other
Southern cities.

After father had completed his college course he went

to Lexington, Kentucky, to study law. On arriving he began to argue with himself that it was absurd to spend months in gaining knowledge of a profession which he did not expect to follow, as he should always have his slaves and hundreds of acres of land to provide him with an income. After traveling several weeks he returned to Mississippi, married mother, who was handsomely provided with property like his own, and settled down to the complacent life of a planter. Although born to that vocation, it was very soon manifest that his heart was not in it. He shut himself up with his books, became a close student of politics, and in 1858 was elected to the legislature, since which time he has been vitally interested in the political life of his state and country.

Father was a fine type of the Southern gentleman of the old régime; in person, tall, slender, well-proportioned, blue-eyed, brown-haired, with delicate, clear cut features, and noble expression; cultured, high-bred, courtly; full of an intense family pride—brave, generous, chivalrous.

The election of Mr. Lincoln in 1860 to the lofty position of president of the United States was regarded by the Southern people as foreshadowing the destruction of slavery. The senators from South Carolina were so impressed with this conviction that they almost immediately withdrew from the national Capital. Legislatures were called in extraordinary session by the governors of the states in the far South for the purpose of devising means of protection from the troubles which they presumed would soon follow. A convention assembled in Jackson, Mississippi, on the 7th of January, 1861, and in two days an act was passed called: " An Ordinance to Dissolve the Union between the State of Mississippi and Other United States with Her under the Compact Entitled, ' The Constitution of the United States of America.' " In short, Mississippi seceded, in an hour freighted with exultant confidence, with tears, with a sense of solemn responsibility. Her national senators, acting on command of the state, retired at once from Washington. Almost every state in the South pursued a course nearly identical with that of Mississippi.

The proposed amendment to the Constitution of the United States, declaring that states would be protected perpetually from the interference of the general government in the maintenance of slavery, was defeated in the Senate. A few months after seven Southern states held conventions and adopted their famous " Provisional Constitution for the Confederate States of America." Belligerent preparations began, followed by the bombardment of Fort Sumter, which brought forth the proclamation of President Lincoln calling for volunteer troops to suppress the insurrection. After that came the civil war which raged four years,—unsurpassed in history for deeds of valor, heroic endurance, terrible suffering and sweeping desolation.

Father was in full sympathy with the leaders of the Confederacy in the cause they espoused. As soon as the first breath of impending strife reached him he began to struggle with military tactics, and was among the first to volunteer. He entered the service as first lieutenant of the Eighteenth Mississippi regiment, and was promoted after the battle of Leesburg to the position of lieutenant colonel. In the spring of 1862 he came home on furlough from Virginia. Soon after returning to his command, he was stricken with an illness of such a serious nature that he was compelled again to retire to the plantation in Mississippi. Commodore Farragut was attacking Vicksburg. The governor of Mississippi called for volunteers in its defense. Father had sufficiently recovered to answer and, going at once to the City of Bluffs, witnessed the first bombardment. When General Sherman made his subsequent movement against Vicksburg, father again volunteered his services.

A requisition had been made by the Confederate government on Southern planters to furnish slaves to build fortifications around Vicksburg. They were sent in vast numbers to do this work which had hitherto been done only by soldiers. Grandfather owned an old negro man, by the name of Moody, who did nothing but make a daily tour of the different residences of the Kearney relatives in the Vernon neighborhood to inquire into the state of health of the occupants, report to grandmother, and in the afternoon to drive up the cows. In his military life father carried a servant with him. On going to Vicksburg the second time he took Moody along to allow the old man to see his sons who were working on the fortifications, as well as to play the role of attendant. It was the last day of the year 1862. My father and his kinsman, James Andrews, a young Confederate officer, were on the train going over to Vicksburg with hearts

on fire and restless with eagerness to be in the midst
of the war. It was a glorious winter afternoon, ripe
with sunshine and balmy with the breath of Southern
winds.

"What a beautiful ride we are having, cousin
Walter!" Just as the words were uttered the engine
was thrown violently from the track. A horrible rail-
road wreck followed, mangling and killing the soldiers,
with whom the cars were crowded, as completely as a
broadside from the enemy's gunboats could have done.
Old Moody escaped unhurt. In wild despair he carried the terrible tidings back to the home of his master.
Bursting into grandmother's room he exclaimed:

"Lor, mistis! Marse Jimmie done killed, and marse
Walter nigh onto daid!"

As soon as the news reached mother she ordered her
carriage and drove as quickly as possible through the
country to the little town of Edwards near which
Moody said the wreck had occurred, and where father
had been removed. There she found him, with spine
injured, three ribs broken, right hand and arm crushed
and raving in delirium. After many wretched weeks
consciousness returned to the maimed soldier; one by
one he picked up the tangled threads of his broken life;
little by little the tide of strength swept in, and he was
carried tenderly back to his plantation home.

Every overture made to the Southern states by President Lincoln, backed by the national government, for
the cessation of armed hostilities was rejected with firm-
ness. In consequence, the Emancipation Proclamation
was issued the 1st of January, 1863. The 6th of March

following, on the plantation at Vernon, my eyes caught their first glimpse of the light of life,—just two months and six days too late for me to be a Constitutional slave-holder.

CHAPTER II

CHANGED CONDITIONS

Our life is always deeper than we know, is always more divine than it seems, and hence we are able to survive degradations and despairs which otherwise must have engulfed us.—HENRY JAMES.

Two more years passed—hideous in bloody strife. The Southern armies, decimated by battle and sickness, were almost destroyed. The Federal forces, overwhelming in numbers, victorious, jubilant, forced their way into every Southern state.

Mississippi was held by them from the Tennessee border to the Gulf of Mexico. Robert E. Lee, with his pitiful band of starving men numbering under 25,000, was entrenched at Petersburg and Richmond. Then came the evacuation, the unwavering pursuit of Grant and Sheridan with their solid lines 150,000 strong, the surrender; 175,000 starved and ragged Confederate soldiers, all told, laid down their arms at the feet of a conquering legion of 1,000,000 men;—and the two armies that had faced each other unflinchingly for four long years melted into civilians with mutual respect and sympathy. Slavery was abolished, and the Southern states were conquered at a cost to the United States of three thousand million dollars and a sacrifice of nearly six hundred thousand lives.

Immediately after the surrender the governor of Mississippi was informed that neither the State government organized since 1861, nor the officers appointed under that government, nor their official acts were recognized by the President of the United States. A command was given to deliver into the possession of the Union armies the public archives and every form of State property. It was done, and Mississippi stood dismantled and dishonored. Every vestige of civil rule was thrust from sight. There was not an executive, not a judiciary; the right of trial by jury was not allowed, nor the writ of *habeas corpus;* there was nothing that bore the semblance of government except martial law which was administered by provost marshals, military commissions and freedmen's bureaus. The negroes had been taken from the fields by thousands and turned into Union soldiers. Those who were left were free, and defied the control of their old masters, as well as made it difficult for officers to bring them under authority. Anarchy triumphed, grinning, red-handed. Desperadoes infested the land. Women were afraid to leave their front doors without being armed or accompanied by a male escort. Wagons were stopped on the public highway and the cotton they were carrying to market to supply the wants of needy families, was forcibly taken. Crime swept like a prairie fire over communities. The constant violations of law were passed by unheeded, unpunished, or the penalties were too feeble to effect fear or prevent recurrence. Industry was dead. "The hands" went to the fields with umbrellas over their heads and resplendent in yellow buckskin

cavalry gloves; they began work when they pleased
and quit when it suited them.   At the same time the
planter was furnishing the land, paying the taxes and
insurance, providing lodging, implements, work-stock,
seed, and giving wages, or a certain proportion of the
crops, stipulated for by contract. He was himself in
the throes of readjustment. His precedents were gone;
he was as uncertain, and almost as helpless as the black
man in the midst of his new and untried conditions.
The land which had been celebrated for its prosperity
was the habitation of wrecks of human beings and ruins
of fortunes. All Southern hearts were smitten with
desolation and gripped with the horror of despair.
Lovely homes had been destroyed. Thousands of persons were on the verge of starvation, and many others
had fled to foreign lands, in voluntary exile. All this
and far more—unutterable—the struggle to maintain
slavery cost the South.

The Federal government, in its emancipation act,
had set afloat an army of aged and infirm negroes who
were perfectly helpless, becoming paupers at once on
receiving their freedom. So in addition to other burdens the white people were forced, in their extremity,
to continue to care for these, as when they were slaves.

As soon as father was physically strong enough to
perform the trying duty, he went to the negro quarters
on his plantation, assembled his slaves, and announced
to them that they were free. There was no wild shout
of joy or other demonstration of gladness. The deepest gloom prevailed in their ranks and an expression of
mournful bewilderment settled upon their dusky faces.

They did not understand that strange, sweet word—
freedom. Poor things! the English language had
never brought to them the faintest definition of liberty
—that most glorious gift of God. They were stunned.
What were they to do Where should they go? What
would become of them? Who would feed and clothe
them, and care for them in sickness, when they went out
from " marster " free?

Noticing their consternation and dumb sorrow, father told them that they might stay and work for him
as hired hands. Some of them did, but the majority
drifted away, and finally all.

The record of the devotion of the slaves to their
owners is deeply touching.

During the war a band of Federal soldiers filled
mother's yard, front and back. Sally, one of the plantation servants, stood calmly surveying them, with
hands peacefully clasped behind her back, while her
turbaned head-handkerchief illuminated the scene. An
officer stalked up to her and demanded to know where
the silver was hidden. With a lofty air of disdain Sally
exclaimed: " Silver! Bless Gord, mister! yo' doan't
know dem white folks! " pointing in the direction of
" the house," as the master's dwelling was always des-
ignated in slave parlance, and where at that time mother
and her little children sat trembling with fear. " Dey
am de *stingiest* white folks yo' ebber sot yo' two eyes on.
Silver! dey ain't nebber had no silver in dere lives!
Got a fine house? Sho 'nuff; but powerful pore inside!
Ugh! *I* ain't see'd no silver *my*self! " Walking off with
infinite disgust, she muttered between her teeth: " Dat

Yankee man sho' am foolish if he thinks I'se gwine ter tell him whar dat silver am!" The officer and his men moved away convinced by her contempt and earnestness. Within ten feet of where Sally stood the silver lay securely buried. She had helped to put it there.

A raid of the Union army was expected through Madison county. Father gave his sword to Aunt Dicey, one of our most devoted allies, and told her to hide it, explaining the reason. No more was thought of it until General Hardee, a Confederate commander, came to the neighborhood to review the troops stationed near Vernon, and who, with his staff, spent the previous night at our home. The next morning one of the officers asked father to lend him a sword, as his own was lost and he did not wish to appear on inspection without one. Dicey was called to bring the hidden weapon. She marched in, bearing it triumphant. The scabbard was rotten and the blade covered with rust. The old woman had buried it.

A year after the slaves were given their freedom they had a great meeting at one of their churches near Vernon. A delegation waited on father to invite him to attend. Having always been a friend of the black race, he accepted their courtesy, although ignorant of the nature of the gathering. On arriving at the appointed place, he found a vast crowd assembled: among them was a body of negro cavalry, charging to and fro with becoming military hauteur. Father was escorted to the platform where the orators of the occasion were seated. These consisted of several Republican white men and one or two black ones. Speaker after speaker was presented to the audience and made flaming orations on the subject of emancipation. It dawned on father, by degrees, that this was the anniversary of the negroes freedom and that he was to participate in its celebration. At last he was introduced without a word of explanation to him or to the black masses in the foreground. Fortunately he had entered into the spirit of the meeting with enthusiasm. With face aglow with emotion of the holiest character and voice strong with a manly and sincere sympathy, he said: " My friends, I honor you for rejoicing over the acquisition of your freedom. If I had been born a slave and the shackles had been broken from my hands I would make every day a time of exultation, and every night upon bended knees would I thank God for my liberty."

The Constitutional Convention of 1865, composed of Southern gentlemen and their sympathizers, met and a universal rehabilitation began.

A horror of negro suffrage was expressed and the convention refused to ratify the Fourteenth Amendment to the Constitution of the United States. However, the Ordinance of Secession was declared null and void; slavery was acknowledged to be dead, and proper adjustment of laws was made.

Then came the days of reconstruction with their attendant terrors. Mississippi was the first to conform to the new order. Other states did not hold constitutional conventions until weeks after hers had adjourned. In the course of the three years following that event the Republican party was dominant in Mississippi.

By order of Congress a constitutional convention

was called which met in Jackson on the 7th day of January, 1868. This body was a motley assemblage. It has gone down in history as the "Black and Tan Convention." It was composed largely of negroes. many of them wholly illiterate, direct from the cotton fields, but belonging principally to the class of barbers, hotel waiters and livery stable hirelings. With the exception of a small sprinkling of Mississippi Democrats the other members were Republican white men from the North; most of whom had failed to command the respect of the people from whose midst they had come,—and who were held in complete disrepute by the Southerners. The entire expense of the convention has been safely estimated at not less than a quarter of a million dollars. A special tax, real and personal, was voted to be levied upon the state, to pay the expenses of the convention.

"The present and all previous constitutions of the state of Mississippi" were "declared to be repealed and annulled." Enfranchising the negro was approved and every effort was made to obliterate the color line in social, civil and political life. Thousands of white citizens of the state had been disfranchised by provisions of the 39th and 40th Congresses; and now the convention of 1868 imposed an additional oath of affirmation on the voters before they would be permitted to express their principles by the ballot.

The taxes levied were exorbitant, apportioned on assessments made at the will of corrupt officials. Land was valued at $100 per acre, which would not have brought $20 if offered in the market. In consequence, millions of dollars worth of property was published under tax sales, which was virtual confiscation. The United States government had placed a tax on all cotton raised in Mississippi. This tax was as high as $10 a bale. Afterward it was disallowed, and an effort was made to secure the refunding of the tax money, which was not accomplished. Imagine the struggle for bread when the people paid a tax of $10 per 500 pounds on the product which constituted their chief means of support!

The Republicans were in the majority in the following legislature. They occupied all the state offices and sent their representatives to Congress. Then began, in full force, the reign of the " carpet-bagger " and the " scalawag."*

B. K. Bruce, the Mississippi negro who afterwards occupied so many prominent positions under the Federal government, was elected United States senator. The lieutenant-governor was a negro; also the state superintendent of education, and other important offices were filled by colored men. Sometimes every member of the board of supervisors was a negro. Under this dark-tinted régime a monument was erected in Jackson by the legislature to the memory of a negro man, who had filled the office of secretary of state.

The Republican legislature of 1870 ratified the Four-

---

* A carpet-bagger was a Northerner who had come into the South with all his possessions in a carpet-bag ; in plain English, a penniless adventurer. A scalawag was a Southerner who deserted his political affiliations for the spoils of the Republican party.

teenth and Fifteenth Amendments to the Constitution of the United States.

Adelbert Ames, of Massachusetts, a son-in-law of General Ben Butler, was appointed military governor of Mississippi in 1868. His administration was characterized by bitter hostility to the whites, which culminated in race riots. The intolerable acts of the governor sealed his doom. Twenty-one articles of impeachment were preferred against him when the legislature of 1876 met and all of them were sustained. He sent in his resignation as governor of Mississippi, which was accepted, and the case dismissed.

Articles of impeachment were also filed against the negro state superintendent of education and the negro lieutenant-governor. The former resigned at once and left the state; the latter stood trial and was found guilty.

The struggle for white supremacy had lasted ten years. The entering wedge for Democratic sovereignty had been made in the autumn of 1875 when, at the election, a compromise had been effected in the way of a division of offices between the Republicans and the Democrats. Regardless of the turn affairs had taken the energy of the carpet-baggers and scalawags fagged not a moment. Night meetings were held with the colored men, in which they were urged to stand by the Republican party as the one that had brought them freedom, and were terrified with the threat of being forced back into slavery if they voted otherwise. With a few rare exceptions the negroes defined freedom as the liberty to be idle. For years they entertained the idea that the lands of the South were to be divided among them—" forty acres of land and a mule, the gift of the Government,"—and they *rested* in that hope. Hordes of them wandered through the country, beating drums and sowing seeds of discontent among those who were peaceably inclined and given to habits of industry. The masses of them were destitute.

The election of 1877 was carried by the Democrats. There was no organized opposition, but every negro knew that he was safer in his cotton-patch than anywhere else. Every man felt that he who would longer submit to the rule of an inferior race deserved to be a slave. Anglo-Saxon blood, North or South, is the blood of free men.

In the enfranchisement of the negro the Federal government laid a heavy curse on the black race. License is not liberty, nor the ballot a blessing unless it has become the expression of a moral principle; and this cannot be until men have been trained to the holy duties of citizenship, and have caught the spirit of an intelligent loyalty to all that for which a righteous government is the standard-bearer.

CHAPTER III

READJUSTMENT

The human soul is like a bird born in a cage. Nothing can deprive it of its natural longings, or obliterate the mysterious remembrance of its heritage.—Epes Sargent.

It seemed impossible for father and mother to realize the terrible change that had come into their fortunes. They continued to live extravagantly for the first few years after the war, keeping the same number of house-servants and giving them exorbitant wages; also to the field-hands who were hired by the month. After awhile the last dollar was spent and the last servant dismissed. The land that had yielded bountiful harvests worked by the slaves, now brought a pittance rented to the freed-men. The struggle for bread became hard both for the laborer and the land-owner. Affairs were growing desperate. Then mortgages were unhappily entered into, and the inevitable failure to meet them was followed by foreclosure. Of all our former possessions only four hundred acres of land, around the old home, were left us.

Among the many destructive agencies to the attainment of independence were the lien laws instituted in the South at the close of the civil war. Before a spool of thread or a pound of flour could be bought on credit

the purchaser had to give a lien on available property—
cattle, horses or land. Failing these he mortgaged his
unplanted crop for supplies during the year. The rate
of interest as well as the merchant's profits on goods
was enormous, usually as high as 100 or 200 per cent.
At the end of the year the buyer found himself in debt
or escaped with only the clothes on his back. Although
the premiums on money have increased, the lien laws
are still in force and are a prime cause of retarded prosperity in the cotton states. One afternoon a young
brother of mine met an old colored man returning from
town, where he had been settling up the year's account
with his merchant. Hearing a half suppressed soliloquy
on the part of the negro, the boy asked: "What is the
trouble, 'Uncle' Willis?"

Without looking up he exclaimed disconsolately: "I
knewed it! I knewed it!"

"Knew what, 'Uncle' Willis?"

"Knewed I warn't gwine ter pay fo' dat mule. I
knewed it all erlong!"

Alas! for "Uncle" Willis, and alas! for thousands
of others who yet know that a penniless state will be the
result of their hard year's labor.

In the midst of the social and financial convulsions
that surrounded us in those sad days, father stood facing the ruin about him with right hand hopelessly injured and depressed continually by a frail constitution.
Mother's health was wretched; she was a martyr to neuralgia. Worst of all, neither of them knew how to
work, nor how to manage so as to make a dollar, nor
how to keep it after it was gained. Children were be-

ing added to the family and sorrows multiplied. My
oldest brother, a boy of brilliant promise, was taken
ill at boarding school and died in his fifteenth year, soon
after returning home. While my only sister was at college in Oxford, Mississippi, she formed a romantic attachment for a young University student, whom she
married when she was but sixteen. Although just five
years old at the time, the memory of that wedding was
indelibly impressed upon my mind: the guests, the
handsome bridegroom, my lovely sister in her bridal
robes, my head aching, and eyes swollen from much
weeping, the good-byes, the roll of the carriage down
the long avenue of cedars to the gate, the after-loneliness
and gloom of the house. Just four years later, when I
returned from school, one afternoon, father folded me in
his arms and sobbing carried me to the parlor where
the still form of my sister was lying in her coffin;—the
child-wife, just twenty years old, and the mother of
two little daughters! Very soon these went away from
us with their young father to establish another home.

The death of my sister left me the oldest child in the
family. There were three small brothers. The iron
entered my soul very early in this great battle we call
"life." I looked about me with wide-open eyes, full
of comprehension and a heart full of bitterness.
Mother's father, William Owens, who had been a Mississippi planter, died when she was a child of ten.
When only three, her mother, a native Kentuckian of
French descent, passed into the shadow-land. Mother
was reared by a married sister who kept her in boarding schools from an early age. She attended an acad-

emy in Nashville and spent her last school-days at the Episcopal Institute for young ladies in Columbia, Tenn. Returning to Mississippi, she married father when she was twenty years old.

Mother was endowed with a strong mind and added to her mental acquirement by constant reading of the best literature. Throughout her book-filled life she has followed national issues and the world's history with keen penetration. She was ever a devoted Methodist and a profound Bible student, a staunch friend, an adoring mother, unselfish, independent in thought and action, energetic in spirit, swift in movement, brief but positive in speech, unswerving in purpose. Her rich brunette beauty made her a belle in girlhood. Though fortified by a nature broad and noble enough to endure bravely many severe strokes of unhappy destiny, yet the loss of her fortune was a blow from which she never recovered. She has lived in retirement, never but once in thirty-four years leaving the seclusion of her home except to attend church, to minister to the sick or to pay an occasional visit to friends in the neighborhood. Like thousands of other heroic women of the South, however, she did not fold her hands in idleness nor weep her eyes blind over the inexorable, but, with admirable courage, went to work. Silk dresses were displaced by cotton ones, the parlor was deserted for the kitchen, the piano for the sewing machine. The *grind* was upon us. We were too pressed in finances to hire anything done but laundry-work and wood-cutting.

When nine years old I put my small "shoulders to the

wheel" to ease mother's burdens. For four years I worked systematically and attended school regularly. Mother's frequent attacks of neuralgia usually prostrated her for a week. On such occasions the cooking and house-work fell to my lot in addition to other duties. If a low moan issued from mother's room early in the morning my heart sank, for it boded no good to me. Hurrying from bed a rush would be made for our old kitchen, twenty yards from the dwelling, very spacious and very uncomfortable, where efforts were begun at once to build a fire in the stove preparatory to cooking. In winter, blowing my hands to keep them from getting numb; in summer sweltering with the heat and fuming with disgust.

Affairs went on in this way for two years. One morning I was trying to get breakfast in a hurry, as it was late, an unusual amount of work was on hand, and my dress had to be changed for school. In attempting to turn some batter-cakes the hot lard splashed on my fingers, burning them cruelly. With a loud cry, I sat down on the floor, folded my hands above my head and rocked to and fro in an agony of body and spirit. Suddenly a light step entered the door. There stood my oldest brother, a little fellow just two years my junior, with an expression of pity strongly tinctured with scorn playing about his half-smiling lips. " Crying, sister? " he asked coolly; " Oh, yes! " was sobbed in reply; " I've burnt my fingers and ruined the batter-cakes, and it's so late,—and there's so much work to be done and get to school. O, how dreadful it is to have to cook! " and the swaying was begun again in despairing misery.

"Sister!" how solemn the blue eyes looked, how dignified the boyish figure. "*Sister!*"—with increasing emphasis—"I have no respect for a girl who is eleven years old and doesn't know how to cook. If you will go into the house I will get breakfast and take it into the dining room." Frantic with delight, but maintaining due outward composure, "Well," I answered, "suppose we make a bargain? If you will cook every time mother gets sick I will tell you one of Dickens' stories or one of Sir Walter Scott's novels as regularly as the nights roll around." "All right! I'll do it!" was the ready assent;—and the compact was sealed. It was never broken.

As the days went by and mother's health failed to improve, and my work failed correspondingly to grow lighter, the younger boys were pressed into service by similar agreements. My second brother was to wash the dishes and help with outdoor labor. The youngest was to do the sweeping as far as his stature and strength permitted. This condition of domestic engineering continued until the time came for me to go away to school. Every night after our lessons were learned for the next day, we gathered around the hearth in mother's room and I told the boys the promised stories; going into smallest details; dwelling on peculiarities of characters, painting minutely their environment, waxing humorous or pathetic according to the situation; all the while watching closely the faces of my auditors. There they would sit for hours, my little brothers, listening intently to every word that was uttered; at times clapping their chubby hands with intense enjoyment, or doubling up their small bodies in convulsive laughter, or holding their lips together with fore-finger and thumb to prevent too boisterous an explosion of hilarity; at other times allowing the great tears to roll down their cheeks, or with bowed heads sobbing aloud. My precious little comrades! They constituted my first audience, and it was the most sympathetic and inspiring that has ever greeted me in all the after years.

One day the announcement was made that a baby had been born in our home, who was to be our brother. The feeling of indignation that swelled into my inmost being surpasses description. Rallying the three boys in the dining-room a caucus was held. Our ages were respectively eleven, nine, seven and five years. I was self-elected chairman on the momentous occasion. "Boys," my voice came trembling with growing wrath, "a child has been born into our family. He will have to be supported. We are disgraced. We were too poor to have any more children. It was just as much as we could do to get along with us four. We must do something to show how angry we are about this baby's coming to add to our troubles." Forthwith we piled all the chairs together in a towering heap and knocked them down by two's and three's, breaking several, and making an awful din. After the fury of the tempest had subsided we met in council again and took a solemn vow never to look at the intruder until we were forced, by unhappy circumstances, to do so; and we never did until we learned that mother was about to die.

A week later Fannie, one of our ex-slaves, came to the rear gallery and said: " Baby! "—all of our ante-

bellum negroes called me " Baby," as I was the last
infant born in the family before the war closed. " Baby,
Mistis is pow'ful bad off an' yo pa, he say ' go fo' de
doctor ! ' " I waited for no further command, nor took
time to search for my sun-bonnet, which was usually
sewed on by mother to preserve my complexion, and as
regularly cut off by some negro woman at my urgent
solicitation, but ran rapidly up the hill to Vernon for
the neighboring physician. On my return, the boys and
I formed a procession and marched into mother's room
with shamed faces and bursting hearts. We were all
nearly grown, however, before we forgave the baby for
being born.

The comradeship begun at the hearthstone with my
three brothers continued. They were ever my most devoted friends and enthusiastic allies. The oldest always
came to my assistance in domestic matters and even
after he had become a man and entered into business
he would give out the meals for me on his visits home,
if mother was ill. He would keep my breakfast warm
if I did not care to arise when the others did, saying
always tenderly, after a gentle tap on my door, " Do
you want to sleep this morning, sister? Very well, I
will attend to everything." We four shared every hardship and rejoiced together in every happiness. In summer we went wading and fishing; the boys chivalrously
taking off their jackets for me to wipe my feet on, and
baiting my hooks. When we were older we went hunting. They carried my gun but I did my own shooting.
Their unselfish acts were returned by me in the intimi-
dation of rowdy boys at school whenever domineering

the little fellows was attempted. In all the association
of our lives my three companions were always loving
and generous to me, never harshly criticizing any action,
however absurd, or the causes I espoused later on,
whether or not they were in accord with the spirit of
them. The affinity between my second brother and myself was most pronounced. We read Shakspeare together, had long walks and confidential talks, discussing
books and life and laying great plans for the future.
We were both ambitious for the widest culture, and as
the chances narrowed, shutting out every hope of a
liberal education we became more closely united in
spirit through our common sorrow. Mother taught my
brothers that as they had but one sister they should
render to her the highest homage,—and they *did,* most
loyally. By degrees every species of rough work of
which they could relieve me was taken from my hands.
If an article was wanted at the table a boy arose to get
it. If a sacrifice was to be endured—an old garment
longer worn—a choice bit of food surrendered,—the
boys undertook the renunciation. Father set them the
example in his exquisite courtesy. His considerateness
for woman never failed him. How sweet that old
home-life was!—the manly gentleness of my brothers,
the royal graciousness of my father, the tender devotion
of my mother!

A law was passed by the legislature of Mississippi
in 1846 establishing a system of public schools. Almost nothing was accomplished, however, up to 1861,
then, of course, the Confederacy absorbed every other
question. In the South generally the attention of the

people was beginning to be drawn toward public education just before the opening of the civil war; but, during the black days of reconstruction there was little inclination to encourage a system of education that would have to be supported for colored as well as white children, the taxes for the purpose being paid by the latter almost entirely. Especially, while the whites were being threatened by the government at Washington with co-education of the races.

The Republican convention of 1868 made provisions for the revival of the system of free schools which went into operation in 1870.

The nearly tax-crushed people objected to an educational law made by a legislature composed of ex-slaves, few of whom could read, and of carpet-baggers and scalawags,—and administered by an alien, non-tax-paying governor and superintendent of education. With such a revival it is marvelous that the free school found any tolerance in Southern life.

Public schools were a costly luxury in those days. The whites paid the expenses of public instruction and, as much as possible, educated their own children in private schools. If a public school teacher had but one pupil he drew his full salary as punctually as if there were a hundred in attendance.

Among my first teachers was a young woman whom mother boarded in order to give me instruction. Her time was divided between reading Byron and drilling me in the multiplication table in vast disproportion. Afterward my public school life began. The patrons of the Vernon school selected a teacher for a certain term, and thought, of course, that the Board of Education, although composed of men of a different political party, would have regard to their opinion and appoint their choice. Instead a strange lady from Maine was given the place. Every parent felt grossly insulted by such a high-handed measure, and refused to send their children to school. Father said he stopped me *on principle*.

I was growing up like a weed, and heard nothing discussed but Republicans. Conjectures began to form in my brain as to what sort of creatures they could be. I heard them called "black," but one day a Northern man, who was said to be a Republican, passed sufficiently near for me to discern that he was as fair as the proverbial lily and shaped like an Apollo. Gradually my cranium cast out its terrifying myths, and reached an adjustment so far as that Republicans looked like other men, but should never be spoken to, and must be shunned like the small-pox.

For a whole term the new teacher went to the schoolhouse, stayed the number of hours required by law, and drew a salary of $75 at the end of each month. She had only one pupil; he was her nephew. The following year the political storm had abated; the Democrats were regaining power. Patrons could now elect the teachers of their schools. The quiet dignity, and superior attainments of the Northern lady had made their impress. Fair play was not neglected when the Southern men's turn came; the patrons who had rebelled and seceded when coërcion was afoot, now selected this same teacher for the next session.

That was the beginning of a bright era for me. As soon as Mrs. Fenderson was met, with her pure, sweet face, and gracious, elegant bearing, my heart was laid at her feet. We became close friends. On rainy days when there would be no pupils at the school-house, but the small nephew and me, my beloved teacher would take us home with her to " hear our lessons." She lived on a plantation not far from ours, with a widowed sister, Mrs. Woodman, whose husband, a colonel in the Federal army, had died soon after coming to Mississippi. They were beautiful women, and so pathetic in their loneliness. It was touching to see how yearningly they reached out after me, only a child, treating me as courteously and as lovingly as if I were a distinguished guest of grown-up proportions. They would talk about their far-away New England home, describing the customs of the people, so unlike the Southerners; show me pictures of noted persons and places; read to me from magazines and attractive books and feed me on delicious " buns " and " cookies," names unknown on a Mississippi *menu*. I began to think there was no spot in all the world so alluring as the dwelling of these friends, nor any human beings as lovely. My first wide outlook upon humanity was gained through them, and they brought to my vigilant soul the awakening of my first inspirations.

Our delightful intercourse and mutual devotion continued without a break until two years later, when Mrs. Fenderson fell a victim to the dread malarial fever. When her tired body was laid away in its last resting place it was in a land of strangers, for unto the end she had lived in unbroken isolation. All the light seemed to die out of life for me. To this day I mourn her loss and revere her memory, with deepest gratitude and with a love unspeakable; but, with Mrs. A. D. T. Whitney, " I believe that there is no away; that no love, no life goes ever from us; it goes as He went that it may come again, deeper and closer and surer; and be with us always, even unto the end of the world."

CHAPTER IV

THE YOUNG LADIES' ACADEMY

There! little girl; don't cry!
They have broken your heart, I know;
   And the rainbow gleams
   Of your youthful dreams
   Are things of the long ago;
But heaven holds all for which you sigh,
There! little girl; don't cry!
           —JAMES WHITCOMB RILEY.

SOON after the close of the war, nearly every old family moved away from the Vernon neighborhood except father's and that of one of his brothers. Three or four worthy, agreeable ones took their places, but the majority of the new-comers were poor, unlettered people, with strong class prejudices and an intense jealousy of the planter-caste. The splendid ante-bellum homes were rented to these and to negroes. Our social circle had pitifully narrowed down. We were literally shut in from the world with nothing to relieve the pressure but books. I read, read, read,—English and American poets, standard fiction, travels, histories, biographies and philosophies. So, in the midst of poverty and desolation, my mind was being fed with the very manna of intellectual life. Reading was done with pencil in hand

33

and note book and dictionary conveniently near. The habit proved invaluable.

Father was struggling heroically with adversity. His first venture at bread winning was in the insurance business; but the returns were paltry enough to make him discard it for the rejected profession of his youth. He studied law, and secured a license to practice in the Magistrates' courts. His clients were poor and troubled and father's missionary spirit so large that the gains from the legal calling were as meagre as from the insurance business; and, after a few years it was abandoned. Agencies for several plantations later fell into his hands and eventually he returned to his planting interests.

The boys soon became old enough to work in the field. Never having been trained as plowmen, their first efforts were crude, developing the most ludicrously crooked rows of corn and cotton. Father was disgusted with the result of their attempts, and, in desperation, took hold of the plow, one spring morning, to teach them precision. " I am ashamed that the outcome of your work is so wretched, after living on a plantation all your lives. Let me show you how to manage a plow!" he exclaimed, grasping the implement with stern determination. It was heavier than he thought— he had never touched one before, and, never after, it is well to add—and the mouth of the mule tougher than he dreamed. Away went the plow! up and down, right and left, here and there; demolishing the serpentine rows and scattering clods and confusion broadcast. The boys were convulsed with laughter, which, however, they wisely concealed. Father kept on trying to conquer the mule and the plow until exhaustion came. Throwing down the lines, he said, very bravely, " Now, boys, you see how it ought to be done. Never let me hear of your failing again! " and walked away with assumed stateliness to hide his crestfallen condition: back to his den and his law books. Dear father! he was born for happier abodes than a Mississippi plantation. The post-bellum world was too much for him. He was not alone in his position. Thousands of ex-slave-holders throughout the South were grappling vainly with conditions that " try men's souls."

My father's youngest brother, " uncle Kinch," as he was familiarly known to us and to the world, had moved from Vernon to Canton; the latter a beautiful town, the county seat of Madison. Here he and his wife, " aunt Henrietta," kept open house in the charming home where they had established themselves. They were both happy-hearted, fond of bright company, devoted to music and blessed with a handsome competency. My aunt had inherited a goodly portion from her father's estate in Louisiana, just after the war, when the cotton planters of Mississippi were enduring terrible financial depression. Uncle Kinch had lost a leg at Cold-Harbor, in the Confederate service, but this misfortune did not imbitter his spirit nor check the flow of his brilliant wit that had descended to him from a long line of Irish ancestry. His captivating jokes and hail-fellow-well-met air attracted the young people in a wide relationship; his home became headquarters for every one in search of a royal time. He had no children: one of his

adopted daughters was married, the other a young lady
in society: but his numerous nieces and nephews were
taken into his affections, all called " honey " and treated
with lavish cordiality. When I reached the age of
thirteen, my public school course was finished. At this
turning point of the way, uncle Kinch invited me to
make his house my home and attend the Young Ladies'
Academy for as long as father would be able to bear
the expense of tuition fees. The hospitality was gladly
accepted. In a few days, my little trunk was packed.
I had been making my own clothes for four years, so
did not go away hopelessly ignorant of how to take care
of myself. Good-byes were said to mother and the boys,
and early one September morning father and I climbed
into the buggy—the carriage had long since been disposed of—with my baggage securely settled at our feet
and, started on the long journey of twenty miles
through the country to Canton. There was at that time
no nearer railway station. Those lonely, lengthy drives,
which were so often enjoyed with father, stand out
prominently in my life's history. It was in these hours
that we had sweet communion and laid the foundations
of an enduring friendship. He talked to me unreserv-
edly of the most sacred things in his experience, and
philosophized upon human existence, upon science, religion, politics, interspersing his remarks with kindly
advice and tender sentiment. Father had the happy
faculty of calling out the best that was in one, and in
turn fascinating his companion with the seemingly lim-
itless resources of his well-stored mind and broad
Christianity. He had always been a companion to his

children, drawing us closer year after year, entertaining us with incidents from the lives of great men and women and of obscure though beautiful characters whom he had known or of whom he had heard, thus inciting us to high aspirations; best of all, holding up before us daily, though unconsciously, the "white flower of a blameless life."

In later years it was a source of intense gratification to me to know that my father was devoid of a suggestion of sectional animosity. He had the highest regard for the true-hearted people of the North and a cordial admiration for their sterling worth and wonderful accomplishments. The civil war left him with a profound respect for the valor of his opponents. He told of their heroism with enthusiasm. After the battle of Leesburg, his company, with three others, was ordered to conduct the prisoners captured to Centerville, Virginia. They left Leesburg at twelve o'clock at night. It was comparatively warm at the start, but by daybreak it had become severely cold. Some time during the following morning, father noticed among the captives a mere youth—not more than sixteen years old—who was without shoes or socks. On inspection it was found that he was nude with the exception of an army overcoat. Upon being questioned, he stated that when the Confederates drove the Union army from the field back to the Potomac, he had pulled his clothes off and jumped into the river with many others to swim to an island where the Federal troops had landed, and where he hoped still to find some of his comrades. "When we got into the river," he said, "the Confederates opened fire, and to keep from being shot, I returned to the Virginia shore. When I looked around for my clothes they were gone." That bare-foot boy, covered only with an old army overcoat, had marched for hours uncomplainingly over the stony roads of Virginia in a temperature at freezing point, while others in the ranks, well-clad, were complaining heavily. Father made an effort to secure some clothing for the young Federal hero, but failing, had him put into a wagon and carried the remainder of the way.

Along with his unprejudiced regard for the Northern people, father cherished an ardent love for the land of his birth and was eloquent over the courage, patriotism and pathetic endurance of the Southern soldiers. Among the numerous instances, illustrative of their unselfish attachment to the cause for which they were willing to lay down their lives, he told, with especial pride, of a noble exhibition of loyalty on the part of a young officer from his own state. While on the Peninsula, near Richmond, Lieutenant Brown, son of ex-Governor A. G. Brown, of Mississippi, the latter at the time a senator in the Confederate Congress, was detailed by the colonel of his regiment to go to Richmond on business for the army. He went to father, who was lieutenant colonel, and asked him to secure his release as the 18th Mississippi was expected every day to enter into an engagement and he did not want the news sent home that he was not in the battle. The young lieutenant could have executed his commission and had a gay time at the Confederate capital, avoiding all the dangers of war, but he preferred to face death in his country's service rather than have his devotion questioned.

Going to Canton with father was not my first separation from home. My aunt and uncle had received many visits from me since my childhood, so it was not hard to go. Besides, I was hungry to be in a school of a high grade, and was willing to suffer to accomplish it. Professor Magruder, a very scholarly man and able teacher, was Principal of the Academy. Associated with him as assistants were two cultivated women. My examinations were safely passed and admission was given to the Freshman class. A solemn mental resolution was taken to make the best of my opportunities. All the force of my intellectual and physical being was brought to bear upon my studies with an energy that knew no stint nor relaxation. Midnight found me at my books, and it was a rare occurrrence for me to go upon the play-ground at recess. Every morning I arose with the sun, wrote a diary of the preceding day and looked again over my lessons.

On Saturdays essays were prepared for the following Friday afternoons. I began to dream dreams of graduation; afterwards of going North to a Woman's College, and later to Germany for further culture in certain branches. Alas! for my fine schemes; destined to premature destruction! After being at the Academy for only two years, father was compelled to take me home because he was unable longer to pay the monthly tuition of five dollars. My humiliation was the most crushing, and my disappointment the keenest, cruelest,

that can come to me in this life. I could not cry. The
fountains of tears were dried up by the deadly east-
wind of despair that was sweeping over me. It would
have been folly to rail at my unhappy fate; it would
only have exhausted my vitality. It would have been
sinful to upbraid father; he would have given me millions if he had possessed so much; he did not have an
extra dollar, and was probably suffering much more
than I. Besides, the boys were growing rapidly, and
the oldest *must* be given at least one year at the University, and every possible economy *must* be practised
to accomplish that object.

*I had never heard of a woman working to pay her
way through school.* Numerous instances of men ac-
quiring an education by hard labor had been related to
me, but never of a *woman.* All the women who were
known to me personally, or through books, or tradition, had their bills paid by male relatives, and made
fancy work, and visited, and danced, and played on
the piano, or did something else equally feminine and
equally conventional, and all were equally dependent
and equally contented,—at any rate, asked no questions.
Industrial institutes and colleges where poor girls could
work their way through were not in existence, and the
doors of the State University, where tuition was free,
were then open only to boys. There was nothing in
Mississippi for young women except high-priced boarding schools and " female " academies. It is humiliating
to women for colleges, academies and boarding schools
established for their education to be called " female."
There is no sex in institutions of learning. The word

" woman " is strong and dignified and suggests courteous consideration. " Female " is weak and almost insulting. It stands now as the exponent of the inferior position of women as early conceptions of the nature and province of women are illustrated in the sculpture and painting of the old masters.

There is a statue in the great cathedral at Pisa representing the temptation of Eve where the serpent has the head of a woman ; and upon the ceiling of the Sistine Chapel at Rome, in Michael Angelo's marvelous production, the devil is painted with a woman's body down to the waist while the remainder of his satanic majesty is in the form of a reptile.

If the thought of *working* to continue my education had entered my brain, which it did not, it would have been throttled at its inception, for my family would have considered it an eternal disgrace for me to have worked publicly. It is true that for four years I had been in a pitiless tread-mill, but it was at home; the world did not know of it; and money, that degrading substance, had not been received for my labor. Household drudgery and public work were very different questions. The former was natural and unavoidable; the latter was monstrous and impossible. I was fairly bound to the rock of hopelessness by the cankered chains of a false conventionality, and sacrificed for lack of a precedent.

Of all unhappy sights, the most pitiable is that of a human life, rich in possibilities and strong with divine yearnings for better things than it has known, atrophying in the prison house of blind and palsied custom ;—

because there is no one in the passing throng brave and great enough to break the bars and " let the oppressed go free,"—into the larger liberty where God meant that all His creatures should *live* and *grow* and *shine*.

CHAPTER V

STORMS OF THE SOUL

We are haunted by an ideal life, and it is because we have within us the beginning and the possibility of it.—PHILLIPS BROOKS.

My early and invincible love of reading, I would not exchange for the treasures of India.—GIBBON.

SINCE the close of the civil war as complete a change had taken place in the South as followed the revolution in France of the latter part of the eighteenth century. Under the new régime which began with the liberation of over 4,000,000 slaves the upper and the middle classes have become amalgamated by the action of the elements of circumstance.

Many of the old families, boasting a long line of descent from blue-blooded and distinguished ancestors, soon were the most sorely pressed financially. Thousands of middle-aged—and younger—men had come home from the last battle-field maimed by wounds or weakened in health by privations. When they entered the gloom of lost fortunes, added to the sorrows of a lost cause, they quickly sank under the triple weight. Hundreds of them were followed to the grave by communities that sorely felt the need of their ripe judgment, their accustomed leadership. The stress of poverty, the paralysis of indolence and the want of purpose benumbed the energies and stultified the pride of other descendants of the old slave-holders, many of whom bore the pitiless stamp of incapacity to wrest success out of new conditions.

The middle classes were equal to the emergency. Adjustment is easier than readjustment. Trained to activities they sprang rapidly to the front, becoming possessors of wealth and leaders in church and state. The inevitable in social life has developed. Marriage into the higher class followed as a matter of course with the middle, for the one wanted prestige and the other money. The distinctions of half a century ago have gradually lost their outlines. The "strenuous life" of the day now engrosses the mind of the Southerner more than the ancient "family tree."

Next to the destruction of caste, the most radical change that has followed in the wake of the surrender of the Confederate armies is that young Southern men and women have learned that work is honorable. Idleness has grown to be a shame. No boy and girl can now hope to realize their highest destiny except through hard, earnest toil of hands or brain. The unsafe and unnatural code of the manorial leisure of other days vanished with slavery. This transition of sentiment, however, has been the slow growth of years. The blossoming "of the tree" whose "leaves" are "for the healing of the Nations" had scarcely begun when my feet stood on the threshold of eager life,—wrestling in strong agony with hopeless but unconquerable purposes.

One of the most unfortunate conditions in all the

world is a state of aimlessness. It saps the springs of power and dulls the finest soul. It drags down and destroys. I was only fifteen. What *was* my future to be? Never to go to the Academy again? Never to attend a Northern college? Never to cross the sea? What *was* there for me to do? How *could* the days be filled so as to keep down the heart-break? Those were the questions that were never stilled. If my life had to be spent on the plantation, and if living meant no more for me than it meant for the women about me, what was the use of reading, of trying to cultivate my mind when it would have the effect of making me more miserable and of widening the intellectual gulf that already stretched between most of the neighbors and myself? What a terrible thing life seemed! And how every impulse of my being hated it with an immeasurable hatred! In those days I died ten thousand deaths. I died to God and to humanity.

From the hour of leaving school in Canton a deadness settled upon my soul. " The door was shut." The night closed in. That was the beginning of an unbelief that haunted me for ten dreary agonizing years. My natural tendency to *questioning* had been intensified by the environments of my childhood; but the spirit of inquiry had not led me further than the human side. The orthodox version of Creator and creation was accepted as credulously as the air that was breathed or the perfume of flowers. It was only the grindings of poverty, the raspings of the jagged edges of every-day existence and the perpetual witnessing of misery in the world about me that caused me first to ask: What is life? Up to the age of fifteen my soul had hoped and prayed and *listened* for the voice of God. I *believed* in Him, and *waited*—not patiently but imperatively,—but —I *believed* and *waited*. In the great storm that engulfed me at that time my faith let go its moorings, and I found myself drifting, without a gleam of light, out upon the waste of midnight waters known as skepticism. As the darkness deepened and thoughts heavy with increasing doubts surged through my brain like a lava-tide, my soul demanded verification for my convictions.

There was no one in the home with whom conversation on such a subject would have been particularly satisfying, so, in desperation a search was made through the library for some book that would answer my queries; but nothing was found touching infidelity except the materialism of certain philosophers. These works were devoured until my mind became saturated with their ideas. I grew to despise Christianity and sneered at every profession of trust in a Supreme Being. Church members were observed critically and every sin and inconsistency which was discovered in them brought out that degree of derision and contempt to which only youth, ignorance and prejudice are equal. Mother had a habit of devoting several hours each morning to study of the Bible. On seeing her surrounded by rows of commentaries and bending over the Scriptures, comparing passages or memorizing texts, I felt my heart hardening, and was conscious of an increased aversion to religion. Our home was headquarters for all Methodist ministers who passed that way, to mother's intense delight and my intense disgust. It was a rule of mine to avoid them whenever possible. My voluntary entrance into the church dated from my twelfth year, during a great revival. Now, when the scene occurred to me I laughed at myself for having yielded to so much emotion, and requested that my name be removed from the church books.

Our home was headquarters not only for Methodist preachers but as well for Democratic politicians. Every candidate for office in the county found his way there, to mother's infinite chagrin and the unbounded delight of father and me. Mother often declined to appear at the table, so I would preside and afterward go into the parlor and talk with the visitors for hours on the situation of public affairs. The aspirants were of all descriptions—from the sleek, town-bred lawyer, " out " for the Senate, to the thin, country granger, who yearned to be a constable. They afforded me ample opportunity to learn the methods of political campaigns and to study the motives and natures of men. Often requests were made by the different candidates for my support in a canvass; but there were others who had little regard for a woman's assistance.

One summer when the roads were kept dusty by the continuous goings to and fro of the anxious office-seekers, one of these interesting subjects dined at our house. He was a most forlorn specimen, with heavy, drooping eyes, straggling moustache and languid movements. His clothes, from the disconsolate set of his collar down to his edge-frayed trousers, draggling over his well-worn boots, gave evidence of a long, hard race on the war path. My sympathies were so aroused that as soon as dinner was over I followed him to the front gallery and, in a burst of condolence, said impulsively: " Mr. F., it is my intention to throw the whole weight of my influence to have you elected! " Looking at me in a sleepily—quizzical fashion, he replied in a droning tone: " It had never occurred to me to ask the assistance of ladies in a political campaign. I supposed they were too busy in other matters to be interested in anything so weighty."

Then he proceeded to tell this joke: There was a great convention of women held somewhere, and a certain local society sent its delegate. When the representative returned a meeting was called that the ladies might hear her report. When this was finished she remarked that questions were " in order." A slim little woman, with a weazen face peering out from a flaring poke-bonnet, arose in the rear of the room, and in a thin, high key called out: " Sister, what sort of hats did the women wear? " Then my hopeful candidate, turning towards me more fully, with a glimmer of something in his eyes which *he* would have called humor, said: " It was my impression that *all* ladies thought more about hats and such things than politics."

It is needless to say the facetious gentleman, with the well-worn apparel and Don Quixote air, lost my support suddenly and completely.

As the days went by they found me more and more deeply immersed in reading. Father bought me translations of the Greek, Latin and Italian poets. An old physician, quite a literateur, who had recently come into the neighborhood, loaned me valuable books that we did not own. He put me under special obligations by sending Allison's " Essays " and Montesquieu's " Spirit of Laws." From other sources some of the works of Ruskin, Carlyle and Herbert Spencer came to me and found an honored place among my treasures. Although applying myself sedulously to books, I was being consumed with a feverish restlessness. My wretchedness went beyond the power of words to express. A deep-rooted desire to do something definite was always present; but every undertaking that suggested itself seemed walled off by insurmountable barriers.

Finally I concluded to study law under father, but when my intention was announced to him he discouraged it utterly, arguing that if there were in my possession the legal lore of Blackstone and the ability of a Portia it would not guarantee me the opportunity of practising in the South. No woman had ever attempted such an absurdity, and any effort on my part, in that line, would subject me to ridicule and ostracism. After this fatal ending to my aspirations, I again sought refuge in books. With no definite object ahead and with not the faintest rim of a crescent of hope above my dull horizon.

*   *   *   *   *

It was the summer of 1878. That terrible scourge, known as yellow-fever, crept relentlessly over the South. For the period of time that it lasted its deadly ravages exceeded the destruction of the civil war. Thousands stood shuddering in " The Valley of the Shadow." Death, grim and awful, stalked through the land knowing no surfeit. It was the blackness of despair. The acme of desolation. Pitiless quarantines were instituted; families were separated by a short dividing line never to be reunited. Others fled in terror from their homes in towns, seeking refuge in tents and cabins; while those who could, went to distant states. Food supplies failed. Hunger, gaunt and hollow-eyed, stole in at the open doors. Men, women and little children moved about listlessly, abandoning all work, looking hopelessly into each other's eyes, wondering, with a speechless fear, who would go out first from among them to return no more. Friends did not visit nor church bells ring. All was silent as the tomb—waiting, waiting, waiting. In the cities, the roll of the death-cart broke the stillness of the streets as it passed swiftly from house to house, collecting the bodies and carrying them to the cemeteries. There was the thud of spades in the earth, driven by men digging grave after grave, but all else was silent—waiting, waiting, waiting. A white woman and her two little children died near us and were buried by a negro man. He dug the graves and, unaided, lowered the bodies into the earth. The husband dared not leave the bedside of the other sufferers in the afflicted family. A physician stopped one morning at the gate to give father a list of fresh victims. In four days the young doctor was dead. A family of ten persons, friends of ours, living near Vicksburg, were all stricken at one time. Nobody dared go near the house but the Italian nurses who had been sent out from the city. As death followed death the plantation bell would be tolled to notify those who acted

as undertakers that another grave must be dug. For
the sake of those still living the dead were lowered in
sheets from the windows, to avoid the slow, ominous
tramp of feet through the hall. All were gone but two
—the father and a young widowed daughter. A
swarthy Dago sat watching the latter, while the blood
settled in her hands and neck. The bell began to toll.
" What is that for? " she asked. " To have your grave
made ready, lady," was the answer.

Late in the autumn the pall lifted. The quarantines
were raised. The refugees returned to their deserted
homes. The voice of traffic was heard. Life waked up
with startled, saddened eyes from her long, deep sleep.
It was the middle of November. Some said that Mrs.
Woodman, our Northern friend, was very ill. Mother
and I walked over the fields to see her. The dying sun
streamed across the faded grass and lay in long, glint-
ing lines upon the distant woods that had many days
since laid aside their summer vesture. The tall rows
of golden-rod and yellow coreopsis that fringed the
winding path swayed noiselessly in the passing breeze.
The houses of the little village, scattered here and there
in a lonely way, had a pathetic mournfulness. Away to
the east a glimpse could be caught of the headstones
that marked the quiet resting place of our dead. The
surrounding country, with its gentle undulations, was
wrapped in unbroken solitude. A peculiar sadness
brooded over all. There is an inexplicable heart-break
in those early days of a Southern winter;—changing
sunshine, shifting shadows and still air full of a mystic
haze.

> " A Spirit broods amid the grass:
>   Vague outlines of the Everlasting Thought
>   Lie in the melting shadows as they pass;
>   The touch of an Eternal Presence thrills
>   The fringes of the sunsets and the hills."

I was peculiarly susceptible to it all at that time, for my soul was full of its vague unrest, its ever present inquiry into life's meaning to me, overshadowed by a grieving unbelief of a Divine Providence.

Soon we were standing in Mrs. Woodman's sick room. As I bent over the bed to greet her, she threw her arms about my neck and, drawing my face close down to her lips, she whispered, " Dear child, I have been so lonely. When I get well you will come to stay a whole week with me, won't you? Ah! if I ever get well!" She sighed and closed her eyes. In an hour she was unconscious. About sunset a happy smile broke over her face and sitting up suddenly she clasped her hands over her heart and cried out joyously, " Here are letters from home! letters from *home!* Oh! I am so glad, *so* glad! " I did not know then the meaning of that cry; but now that it is given me to see clearly and not " through a glass, darkly," a realization comes that the " letters from home " brought the blessed call from her Lord, " Arise, let us go hence " where " there shall be no more death, neither sorrow, nor crying, "—neither suffering nor loneliness,—where the " many mansions " are—in the " city which hath foundations whose maker and builder is God." The next day the tender, beautiful friend of my childhood was dead,—*from yellow fever.*

CHAPTER VI

A NEGRO SERMON

Are you in earnest? Seize this very minute;
What you can do, or dream you can, begin it!
—GOETHE.

THE following January, I went to Canton to visit
my uncle's family. While there an unusually cheap ex-
cursion to New Orleans was offered by the railway. I
had never been to a city and had all of a girl's eagerness
to see one; especially our flowery, fascinating, dear,
dreamy Crescent City. In a letter to mother the fact
was mentioned that a number of my friends were going
to take advantage of the low-rate trip, and expressed
the wish that such a joy were possible for me. In a few
days father came to Canton, and handed me a package
and a crumpled note. On opening the latter I read:

" DEAR SISTER: Mamma tells me that you want to
go to New Orleans. I send you $15.00—part of the
money that came from the bale of cotton I raised last
year.
                              " Your Affectionate Brother."

My loyal sympathizer in house-keeping sorrows thus
opened the way for me to go. So, unexpectedly and
gratefully, I made one of a party consisting of a gentle-

man and his wife and two young ladies besides myself.
After being comfortably located at a hotel we entered
upon the usual sight-seeing. As we went from point
to point, to the amazement of my chaperones nothing
astonished me. All things were surveyed without a
ripple of excitement or surprise. I had read of or heard
" the sights " of New Orleans discussed until my imagination was familiar with them. The French market
with its delicious coffee and chocolate; the picturesque
bend of the great river bearing upon its breast the huge
ships from foreign waters; Canal street with its wonderful breadth, Clay's statue and everywhere beautiful
women; Jackson Park, and its equestrian bronze of the
old general who " fout the Britishers; " the street-cars,
the opera-houses, the handsome residences were as
thrice-told-tales to me.

My love of adventure and spirit of enterprise led me
to separate myself from my party, while visiting the
mint, and to go in search of some relatives in a distant
part of the city. The most explicit directions were
given, the right car was boarded and the desired
street reached, but at a point far beyond the number
wanted. While nervously going backward and forward
scanning doors, footsteps behind were heard coming with a persistence that made me know I was followed. In a flash the remembrance came into my mind
of all that had been told me of country girls being
gagged, chloroformed and murdered on their first visits
to cities. A scream was in my throat when the man
reached my side. Instead of a ruffian, a courteous voice
said: " May I take the liberty of helping you find the

number you are evidently in search of? I too am a stranger in the city and am experiencing some of its difficulties." It is said that dogs and children are fine judges of character. Many women also do not outgrow this elemental power. Without an instant's hesitation his aid was accepted. In a few moments the right house was reached and the gentleman had presented his card, bowed and walked rapidly away. I read " J—— W—— B——, Attorney-at-law, Philadelphia, Pa." This incident set two thoughts germinating in my brain : The interdependence of human beings, and, That humanity will bear trusting; it responds according to the faith put in it. Wider experience has convinced me of this more and more largely.

*   *   *   *   *

Since gaining their freedom, the negro women's natural love of dress has developed inordinately. It is one of their strongest predispositions—rivaled only by their religious emotions. Those about us bought brilliant-hued stuffs and had them made with most bizarre effects,—a favorite being bright yellow calico trimmed with blue. Red was at a discount as it made them think of " hell-fire," they said. They were ignorant of sewing except of the plainest, coarsest order, so they paid to have their " Sunday-go-to-meetin' " dresses made. My desire for employment was so great, and there being no other opening, though it nearly crushed me, I swallowed my pride and asked the negroes to bring their sewing to me. They did it cheerfully. Day after day they came bearing their precious bundles, and, finding their way into mother's room, which was the scene of all our labors, would drop them on the floor and stand until negotiations were concluded. None sat in our presence. There has always been a very nice adjustment of this point between the families of ex-slave-holders and negroes; the latter have a fine sense of when to accept or refuse an offered chair. It would be useless to explain it. "Oue must be born to it" to understand, as is said in South Carolina about cooking rice properly.

The old servants usually began with "Mistis, how old I is?" When told they would invariably give vent to their surprise by an ejaculation beginning in a long, high-keyed crescendo and ending in a diminuendo as abrupt as it was full of softest musical rhythm. "Lor', mistis, yo' say I is! Marster, he done put it down in de book fo' de surrender, but I sho fergits it."

The age of the negro always seems a puzzle to him, and judging by his face alone, is a problem impossible of solution, for he may be sixty-five or eighty-five, twenty or thirty. In old slave days the master kept an accurate record of their ages. How many generations of care-taking for themselves will be needed to register the true flight of time on their cheerful, unreflecting faces as it is recorded in white features, not by years but by the thought and responsibility and the spiritual force of the life?

The younger women introduced their business with, "Miss Belle, I done brung yo' a dress fer to make fer me. I has all de needfuls excusin' uv de fread. Ef yo' will gin me dat, I'll bring yo' some aigs nex' time I come." In sewing for the negroes mother did the cutting and fitting and all of the hand work; I did the stitching, bending over the machine week after week, until my back ached and my eyes grew dim from the awful strain. These dresses were often ruffled to the waist and otherwise elaborately trimmed, for which we charged only fifty or seventy-five cents. By this means we helped to " make both ends meet."

One of the most popular places for the exhibition of all this gaudy apparel was the church, especially during protracted meetings. These are still the chief diversion, beginning as soon as crops are " laid by," in July, and continuing until the cotton picking season opens in September. The services, always at night, are indefinitely extended until near daybreak. In dimly lighted, meagrely furnished frame buildings vast crowds gather. In the pulpit with the preacher is the precentor—not known by that name—some brother of noted devotional gift who begins the service by " lining out " a hymn, his voice intoning and dimly suggesting the tune with which the congregation follows,—one of those wild, weird negro airs, half chant and dirge, so full of demi-semi-quavers that only the improvisator-soul can divine it, yet, so full of strange, sweet melody and pathos, rendered in their marvelously tuneful voices, it is no wonder a suppresssed emotion begins to communicate itself through the audience. Fiery prayers increase the spiritual temperature. These are full of pathos and frequently close with: " Please, Sir, Lord Jesus, do dis

here thing what yo' pore ole sarvant ax yo' fer." Ejaculations, groans and a measured tapping of heels on
the bare floor becomes general.

Snatches of song and more prayers prepare the way
for the sermon. Words cannot picture the fervor of it,
the facial expression, the wild, funereal cadences of
voice.

One that I heard during March, 1899, in one of the
earliest settled and most cultured parts of Mississippi,
was preached by a typical African, very black, much
white in his prominent eye, long under jaw and the inside of his hands a light cream color. A favorite ges-
ture was to hold the palms out, towards the audience.
He wore a clerical black suit, but around his neck, just
under the coat collar, a flaming red scarf appeared, the
ends hanging over his waistcoat. The occasion was the
funeral of a respectable colored man, Felix Jackson,
who had died on the plantation which I was then visiting, and whose body was in front of the pulpit.

The preacher began by saying, " I doan' fool my time
'way much er preachin' funeral sermons. I'se got sum-
phin' better to do in dis here worl'. I'se in er sing'ler
persishun here ter day. Yo' all is Baptis' an' I is Meth-
odis'; but I think I can prove dat my doctrin' is de
correc' one. I done studied all de ologies wid dat eend
in view. I been studied geology, an' zoology, an' soci-
ology, an' ethnyology, an' Christianology. I'se read
Demosthenes, an' Cicero, an' Plato, an' Moses, an'
Josephus an' Jehosaphat an' all de udder translaters er
de Bible. But all dat ain' here ner dar; it doan' 'mount
ter nothin' in der presence er yer daid an' when yer

think er de jedg'men' day, (whining) Brer Felix Jackson doan' cyar no more 'bout it. He done gone whar yer cyan't go wid 'im; er—er—(groans). Yer'll neber see 'im no more er follerin' behine he mule in der fiel'; yer'll neber see 'im agin er comin' 'long der road ter dis here church; yer'll neber see 'im gwine inter his house ter his wife an' little chilluns when de day's wuk's done (moans, screams).

"Brer Felix Jackson's body's in dat coffin 'fore yer. But *he* ain' dar! O—oh! *No!*—L-o-rd! He done *rise!* He done rise wid taller (pallor) on his face (shrieks), to meet de 'possle Matthew, an' de 'possle Mark, an' de 'possle Luke, an' de 'possle John. An' ebry one on 'em say, 'Felix Jackson, what yer been doin' in de life yer jes' lef?' Oh! *Lo-r-d!* brudderin' dat's er solem' momen'! (groans). Got ter face de 'possles an' 'count fer yer deeds done yere on de yearth! Ebry one on 'em knowed 'im, dough he ain' take his body wid 'im. De Word say what some folks kin go to glory widout dyin' —translated dey calls it. But brudderin, *I* say whedder yo' dies er yer *doan'* die, *somewhar* betwix dis worl' an' de nex' yer *got* ter lose de body. Our daid brudder done got ter de presence er der angel Gabrell, an' Gabrell he say, 'Brer Felix Jackson, *what* yer been doin' in de udder worl'?' But de angel know, an' Brer Jackson know, he kin gib er good 'count er *his*self. Brer Jackson ain' got no taller (pallor) on his face *den*. De angel done tech it wid glory, an' glory ter God! he go right in! (shouts).

"But what yer niggers gwine ter do when yer stan's whar Brer Jackson done stan'? What yer gwine ter

do when yer's on yer coolin' boa'd lak he done bin?
What yer gwine ter answer when yer call on fer yer
sins what yer done while yer's awalkin' aroun' ? Some
er yer say dar's white sins an' dars black sins; but doan'
fool yerselves! Dar ain' no meaner sinner ner a nigger
when he *gits* ter sinnin'; an' sin is sin whedder it's
white folks' sin, or black folks' sin; an' yer got ter quit
yer meanness if yer eber means ter git ter glory. (Yes,
Lord!); fer de trumpet'll be er soundin' an' de jedgmen' day'll be on yer lak' er thief in de night. Whar'll
yer be, sinners, when de graves is er openin' an' de daid
is er risin? (Eyes rolling, palms out.) O—Oh! *L-o-r-d!*
whar'll yer be when Brer Jackson'll be er risin wid er
boa'd (board—his coffin lid) ober his face! Whar'll yer
be *den!* er-er-er!" (Wild excitement.)

Women sprang to their feet with unearthly screams
and began to rend their clothes, upon which other sisters, whom " the Sperit had not got " *yet,* held the fren-
zied hands. Some went into trances and fell on the
floor; others grappled with the shouters, trying to " hold
them down." Failing in this they laid them on their
backs and sat upon them.

During all this violent demonstration the preacher
continued his sermon, gradually cooling down his hearers. The men did not shout, but sat with the " holy
laugh " on their faces, ejaculating fervently, tapping
their feet in metre, and under as intense, if less noisy,
excitement as the women. The trancers stayed where
they fell until they regained consciousness; then they
related with wild inflection and gesticulation what the
angel Gabriel had " done tole 'em " while their spirits

sojourned between heaven and earth. My friend and I sat surrounded by the distracted multitude trembling with fear, not knowing what moment we would be stunned by a blow or crushed by a falling body. When the climax of wildness was reached, a family servant of my hostess pushed her way to us through the struggling throng and touching my companion on the shoulder said: " Miss Hattie, yo' an' Miss Belle had better leave. It's er gittin' dangerous here." We beat a hasty retreat and did not feel secure until we were once again under the sheltering roof of the old plantation home.

At the close of the protracted meetings the baptizings begin. Multitudes assemble on the banks of a pond, or creek, or river, and the candidates are led out into the depths by the pastor and the deacons. It requires a heavy squad for the shouters are more unmanageable in the water than in the church. Some of the members are baptized twice in successive years as their conversion is found not to be genuine the first time.

It is customary among the colored people to preach the funeral sermon of a deceased church member or relative several weeks, or even months, after the death, —just as is convenient. These are particularly prominent occasions, calling for extra " finery " and parade. Everybody who can afford it is newly gowned, and the " siety " to which the departed friend belongs is conspicuous. The society in the church represents the club-spirit of the negro. The wife of the deceased is permitted to sit as chief mourner at the funeral sermon, provided she has not married again before that ceremony. In the event, however, that another spouse has been taken, and she had yet had the effrontery to occupy the chief seat, the deacons lead her in shamefacedness and deep disgrace to the rear of the church. The same rule applies to the husband of " de ceasted."

Some of the widows are gay indeed. One of uncle Kinch's ex-slaves, a few years ago, went to Canton on business and called to pay her respects to my aunt. In course of conversation the latter asked: " What is the news down at Vernon, Hester? " Stuffing her hand-kerchief into her mouth to prevent an explosion of laughter, she giggled out hysterically, " Nuthin' strange, Miss Henretter! Jes' my husban' die las' week! "

One day I asked an old colored woman who was doing house work for us, " aunt Burley, how many children have you had? " " Nineteen," she answered laconically. " How many have died? " was my next question. " All but two," she replied. " You have been unfortunate, aunt Burley," was my sympathetic re-joinder. " Ugh! chile! I think I'se been pow'ful lucky! she exclaimed with a triumphant shrug of her shoulders and a satisfied twist of the ends of the ban-danna handkerchief that adorned her woolly head.

In negro life, as among all lower races, the woman is the slavish subject of the man. It used to be declared on a plantation, after the war, that the only man who did not whip his wife was the man whose wife whipped him. It was said to be pitiable to see these wives come to the old master for protection. " I want yo' to make Zeke stop beatin' me, marster! I can't stan' it no longer!" one would complain. "I don't see what I can do," would be the answer. "I have no authority; he is as free as I am. You will have to go to the Freedman's Bureau about it." "What I got ter do wid de Bureau! Yo' allers did 'low dat he shouldn't whip me when he b'longed ter yo'!" All that a planter could do under the circumstances was to threaten to put the man off his place; but this did not remedy the evil, for, if he left, he took his family with him.

The tyranny of the husband over the wife largely destroys the sacredness of the unity of the two lives, and brings marriage into disrepute. A negro woman, who is the mother of several children although unmarried, upon hearing of the wedding of a colored girl living on the plantation of a friend of mine in Louisiana, exclaimed scornfully: "Dat nigger sho was er fool ter git married! she doan' know what trubble she is er gittin' inter. I allers sade I was er gwine ter be er ole maid an' I is!" A most appalling looseness of morals exists among the negroes.

Recently an investigation was made into the causes of the excessive death-rate of the colored people. This inquiry was conducted under the supervision of Atlanta University, assisted by graduates from other colleges and universities for the higher education of the negro, such as Fisk, Berea, Lincoln, Spilman, Howard and Meharry. Conferences were subsequently held to ascertain the social and physical condition of the race. After a close study of the question, involving accurate comparisons of statistics gleaned from different cities, and a personal visitation to the homes of numerous negroes, it was declared that this mortality is not the result of diseases produced by unsanitary surroundings, but is due to the colored people's "disregard of the laws of health and morality." Valuable papers were read, entirely void of race prejudices, making a frank acknowledgment of the degradation of the blacks, and expressing an earnest desire for remedy. Eugene Harris, of Fisk University, one of the most broad-minded negroes attending the conference, stated: " The constitutional diseases which are responsible for our unusual motality are often traceable to enfeebled constitutions broken down by sexual immoralities. This is frequently the source of even pulmonary consumption, which disease is to-day the black man's scourge.

"According to Hoffman, over 25 per cent of the negro children born in Washington City are admittedly illegitimate. According to a writer quoted in Black America, ' in one county of Mississippi there were during twelve months 300 marriage licenses taken out in the county clerk's office for white people. According to the proportion of population there should have been in the same time 1,200 or more for negroes. There were actually taken out by colored people just three.' James Anthony Froude asserts that 70 per cent of the negroes in the West Indies are born in illegitimacy. Mr. Smeeton claims that ' in spite of the increase of education there has been no decrease of this social cancer.' "

It should be remembered that a race, like an individual, has its period of youth. The African in America has not yet advanced beyond that age. We must not expect too much of him at once. It has taken many centuries to bring the Anglo-Saxon to his present imperfect ethical development. It will not take less time to perfect the negro,—and whoever reckons for him without considering the thickness of his skull and the length of his under jaw, the relative smoothness of his brain and the amount of gray matter at his nerve centres will be disappointed.

It is higher ethical training from the pulpit and in the schools that the negro needs. He likes a preacher and a teacher of his own color. While this is well in that it gives him a leader near enough to his own level to be in sympathy with him, it has the disadvantage of depriving him of close and constant contact with the standards to which an African *must* come, if he survives in an Anglo-Saxon civilization.

This is the " negro problem "—part of it. What shall be done with it? " The slow process of the ages " is the message that comes to our reflection. Meanwhile those who care,—and there are many in the South who do,—vote more money for the public schools, and help the negro to build his churches, and *wait*—because they do not see what else to do. The end of another century will be time enough at which to take the next reckoning of what American civilization has done for " Our Brother in Black."

CHAPTER VII

A HIGHER LIFE

Rather the ground that's deep enough for graves,
Rather the stream that's strong enough for waves,
   Than the loose sandy drift
Whose shifting surface cherishes no seed
Either of any flower or any weed,
   Whichever way it shift.—ANON.

WHEN I was sixteen years old an invitation was received from some relatives in Oxford, Mississippi, to attend the Commencement exercises at the State University. This was my first entrance into society as a young lady. My wardrobe consisted of inexpensive Swiss and organdie dresses trimmed with some old laces that mother had rescued from the wreck of time. My appearance was that of a woman and long since the decision had been made, to " put away childish things." My girlhood griefs were buried out of sight.

The desire of my heart had been to lead the life of a thoroughly independent creature; but I soon found that it seemed absurd to differ from other persons. Now there was nothing to do but drift with the tide. I laughed and talked and acted like the women about me; but there was a sting in it all to which the world was not blind. My society chat had a current of sarcasm, my merriment a tinge of bitterness. A knowledge of card-playing had been gained while attending school in Canton, and my first lesson in dancing was taken in such extreme youth that it is impossible to recall it. During Christmas holidays there were always several parties given in the neighborhood of Vernon, and in summer there were numerous out-of-door festivities. I attended them all and often danced through a winter night and a long, hot summer day when not over ten years old. Dancing was a part of a Southern girl's education. It was as natural as eating or laughing. After a young lady had made her debut, she would soon become " a wall-flower " in society if she did not dance. On going to Oxford it was an easy thing for me to fall in with the trend of custom. The days were divided between playing croquet with the University students and returning fashionable calls; the nights were given to games of euchre and attending entertainments.

The last and greatest social function of the season was the Commencement ball. Mother had unearthed an old ante-bellum blue silk and put it in my trunk for an emergency. This was now brought forth and laboriously transformed into an evening costume. The stains of years were covered up with the inevitable lace or hidden by sprays of flowers. My escort called at ten o'clock in a carriage with another youthful couple and we went to the ballroom. The dignified custom of chaperonage was then nearly obsolete. My program was filled out and I danced straight through it until the last strain of music ended with the advent of the sun next morning. With me nothing has ever been done by halves. Whatever has been undertaken at all has been undertaken with intensity.

The summer at Oxford was the beginning of gaieties that continued, almost without interruption, for three years. The winters were spent at my uncle's home in Canton and in Jackson with very dear cousins. Another visit was made to New Orleans under happier circumstances. In summer my friends visited me at the plantation. While in the country we rode on horse-back, had buggy drives and out-door games; went on fishing and camping excursions; attended picnics and barbecues; gave dinners and teas, and exchanged visits with two delightful families who had guests with them throughout the warm months. These families and ours had only recently become acquainted as they lived miles away from us; but distances are small considerations when "life is new" and pleasure the one pursuit in existence.

My stays at home were comparatively brief during these three years; but while there my reading was continued and mother and I managed to do a great deal of sewing for the negroes. My oldest brother had one year at the University and immediately after secured a position in a mercantile establishment in the northern part of the state. During my visits to the towns there was a ceaseless round of balls, theatres, receptions and card parties, nearly every one of which I attended; from the Governor's inaugural entertainment at the Mansion to an impromptu dance in a private home.

Those were fateful months. The foundations of ill-health were laid which haunted me for fifteen years.

Often in freezing weather my thick shoes and heavy clothing were put aside for thin slippers and gauze dresses and bare neck and arms. After dancing till heat or fatigue became unbearable a rush would be made into the deadly night air, with only a filmy lace shawl thrown over my shoulders for protection.

There were few days in those three years in which I did not have a desperate fight with my soul. Conscious of not living up to my high conceptions of life, I hated myself and abhorred the way my time was spent. The truth forced itself upon me that theatres were rarely elevating, that the trail of the serpent was over every card, that round-dancing was demoralizing and that many of the young men who danced with me were not worthy of my friendship. Night after night on returning from an entertainment, I have sat before the fire pouring out my contempt for myself and all *my* world in scathing denunciation, always ending with the moan that had been in my heart since childhood, " What *is* there for me to do? Life is so empty, so unsatisfying! I wish I had never been born! " The girls who kept the vigils with me would greet my torrent of grief and rebellion with peals of laughter. Bessie Fearn, my cousin and constant companion, a most brilliant and fascinating young woman, would say, " It is impossible for me to understand you. How *can* you see any harm in cards or dancing or theatres? I am as untouched in spirit to-night as a child could be! " In later years, when a personal knowledge of Christ came to her, these things in which she once saw no " harm " palled upon her and in renunciation of them her life became a glad song of consecration until the time came of " entering into rest " where her eyes beheld " the King in his beauty " in " the land that is very far off."

After the last fierce struggle with the finer elements of my being, a definite determination was made to *abandon* the shallow, aimless life that had been entered upon;—and it was *done,*—suddenly and forever. It was concluded further that I must go to work, that an occupation uplifting and strengthening must be secured if every family tradition was shattered and if my life were forfeited in the attempt.

Father and I had always been congenial except along certain lines. In the light of after experiences we both became wise enough to avoid all splitting issues. Up to this time, however, the depths of his convictions concerning work for women had never been sounded. Mother believed in me utterly. She was my devoted, changeless, unquestioning ally. Father, on the contrary, with all his gentleness and affability, was a severe critic and, at times, a most sarcastic opponent. Consequently, whenever an embryo scheme was on hand, he was invariably sought in order to get an expression of opinion, regardless that his views might be totally different from mine. When a child rest never came to me until every important occurrence of my daily life had been related to him, heedless of the consequences of the confidence.

He had been terribly grieved over my indulgence in round-dancing. At the country festivities, I had been allowed to attend in childhood, only the dignified quadrilles of earlier times were in vogue. It had not occurred to him that my inclinations might reach out

tendrils towards the customs of my own day. He had
often tried to dissuade me from round-dancing, but
was unable to extract a promise that it would be given
up. However, when my decision was reached to dance
no more I went at once to him and announced it. " Well,
my daughter," he remarked, surveying me calmly,
" you do not deserve a particle of credit, for you do not
stop because it is right, but because you are disgusted."
This diagnosis of the case was accepted, but with a
tremendously offended ego.

Soon after this encounter, father was again inter-
viewed. Broaching the subject abruptly I said: " Life
has grown very tiresome to me and some change *must*
be effected. It is my intention to work at some employment that will make it possible for me to support
myself." Father looked at me a little dazed, and answered: " Work?" with a high-tide inflection on the
word. " *Work?*" with renewed emphasis—" and may
I ask of what nature your work will be?"

" Certainly," was my quick reply, " I intend to teach
school." " *In*deed!" said father, with a peculiar drawl
of the prefix which would have sent terror to my soul
when a child.

" Yes, sir!" came my answer with decision, " I am
going to teach school."

" But you forget," he exclaimed, making a desperate
effort to control the quaver in his voice and to hide
the tremor of his eyelids that revealed the storm in his
heart, " you *forget* that I am able to give you a support.
You forget that you are my only daughter. Do you
mean to tell me that you are going to teaching? I will

never consent to it!"—and he walked off with an air which told too plainly that the conference was ended.

Without being in the least dismayed, and saying not a word to any one, I put on my sunbonnet and gloves and started forth determined to settle the school question. There were few children in the immediate neighborhood and the majority of these were very poor; but wherever there was a shadow of a chance for success, their homes were visited and a request made for pupils. An upstairs bedroom in our dwelling was transformed into a schoolroom, and the following Monday morning I entered upon my career as teacher. Father did not say one word. His courtesy was never at fault; besides, he had discovered in me a certain will-force, inherited from both "sides of the house," and an indomitable energy which he began to respect. At the end of the term he said to me: "Allow me, daughter, to congratulate you upon your fine success." Mother was radiant with delight from the beginning, for she understood my longings. Everything was made to bend to my wishes. The children were permitted to eat their lunches on the long front gallery upstairs, and to romp in the yard under the closely matted branches of the great cedars and among the trailing periwinkle vines whose green leaves carpeted almost every foot of ground. There were only seven pupils in my school and their tuition fees amounted to but $12 a month; but those twelve dollars were as large as twelve full moons in my eyes and as precious as blood-drops. Among the seven children there was only one at all well advanced; while teaching him I had a good chance to review text-books and to again get into the habit of study. While managing the others an excellent opportunity was afforded for the cultivation of the grace of patience, which was sorely needed, and of gaining some practical knowledge of the methods of teaching.

I was nineteen years old at the beginning of my little private school

CHAPTER VIII

THE PUBLIC SCHOOL MA'AM

> Nothing's small!
> No lily-muffled hum of a summer bee,
> But finds some coupling with the spinning stars;
> No pebble at your feet, but proves a sphere;
> No chaffinch, but implies the cherubim;
> . . . . . . Earth's crammed with heaven,
> And every common bush afire with God.
> —ELIZABETH BARRETT BROWNING.

At the close of my private school session a determination was made to expend my energies no longer on so few children and with such small financial returns; but that an application should be made for the public school where there would be more pupils and a larger salary. Once more my plans were revealed to father. His amazement and opposition were greater this time than before. "Teach the public school!" he echoed after me. "The *public* school!" incredulously. "Why, I would not have you brought in contact with its rougher elements and subjected to dictates that would surely come, for all the world! A little private school in the seclusion of our home was a different matter entirely. Nothing could induce me to consent to your going out as a public school teacher."

74

The next day I called on the trustees of the public school at Vernon and asked to be their teacher for the autumn term. They were astonished, but readily consented. Keeping my own counsel, one of my brothers was induced, in the course of a week, to drive me to Canton where a call was made on the County Superintendent of Education. With straightforwardness I said, " Mr. S, it is my intention to support myself. You will oblige me forever by granting me a first-class certificate for a public school without requiring an examination. It has been over four years since my school days ended. It would be impossible for me to stand an examination; but it is equally certain that I am competent to teach the Vernon school and make a success of it." The superintendent smiled indulgently, filled out a certificate and handed it to me. The law then in reference to examinations was not as rigid as now.

With a joyous spirit my face was turned homeward and my official document was displayed with all the pride of a conqueror. At the opening of the fall term I was seated in my chair of state viewing with satisfaction the half hundred boys and girls who greeted me. They were of all shapes and sizes; from young men with beards on their faces to roly-poly urchins just out of bibs. Oh! what a time we had! The boys chewed tobacco during school and spat upon the floor. Every now and then an especially genteel fellow walked to the nearest window to expectorate. The girls were piously and prettily demure while they thought I was looking at them; but the instant my gaze was removed they threw spit-balls at the infant class and love notes to the giant rustics who were wrestling with their quids and slates.

They were unclassified; there were not ten books among them which were alike. The grading was found to be an unending task, for every week there was a new set of pupils. The children in the different families took turns in doing the work and resting from their mental labors. Before the close of the session, however, several solid classes had been formed and impressed with the importance of attending school regularly. These stood by me to the end and delighted my heart by making rapid progress.

The struggle with the "submerged tenth" continued. There were fights among them at recess and while going home in the afternoon. Some of the girls swore like troopers and the boys struck them for it. Only my presence in the midst of the hordes prevented rough language and blows. Court was held as regularly as school and justice administered according to testimony.

It was impossible to use my judgment in selecting studies for the pupils as their parents bought the books that suited them and refused to get others. One day a boy handed me a note from a patron which ran as follows: " Mis I doant warnt mi Sun ben To studdie Nuthin but reedin wrighten spelin and Figgers Respecfuly Willium L——."

A terrible strain on my patience was realized in teaching a fat, little, five-year-old boy his alphabet. It seemed impossible, after all the other letters were conquered, for him to learn " u." Seizing his chubby hand in mine, the invincible character was written in his palm with a piece of chalk. Then holding it before his eyes I said, " Now, John, this is u." Puckering up his face as if in mortal agony he gave a loud yell that ended in a heart-broken wail, and sobbed out, " No, Miss Belle, dat ain't me-e-e-ee! "

Some of the boys were manly, home-spun fellows with imagination. One of them, on a memorable morning, was given the word squirrel to spell and define. Tom rattled the spelling off in grand style with startling vehemence. Then came a dead pause. Looking up I said : " Well, now, the definition? What is a squirrel? " " A varmint." " Oh! that won't do! Try again. What is a squirrel? " " Somethin' what runs up a tree." " No, sir! that won't do. Try again. What is a squirrel? " A long pull at his " gallusses," a puzzled searching of the ceiling with a look that suddenly broke into light, then a glad shout: " Oh! I know! A squirl's somethin' what eats nuts with his tail standin' up! "

When the spring opened all the large boys had to stop school to work in the crop. My salary depended on the number of pupils in attendance, dropping some months as low as $18.00, and never going beyond $25.00—the daily attendance ranging from five to fifty. Regular visits were made to all my patrons in the effort to inspire them with the importance of educating their children. Poor little homes were entered and parents met who had lived within two miles of our plantation since my early childhood, but who were unknown to me. At first this was an ordeal, but by degrees my interest in the children deepened, and the poverty and ignorance of their home-protectors became a positive burden on my soul; profound pity began to push out less noble feelings.

Those were days of quiet growth for me. In that little school-house, which was not more than a hut, among those rude girls and boys was learned my first real lesson in self-command. In the beginning there was a fire of insubordination smouldering in the hearts of even the meekest looking of my undisciplined rabble that only needed a spark to set it into a blaze. There was one particularly mild-mannered boy, with large, dreamy eyes and the languid air of a " Vere de Vere." He never knew his lessons. Finally my patience reached its last gasp and I told him if he failed the next day he would have to suffer punishment. He was utterly deficient and was called forward. Thrusting his hand into his pocket and drawing out a large, open knife he struck at me. My movements were quick enough to seize his wrist and divert the blow, and my hands were strong enough to wrest the knife from his grasp. He was dealt with, after the Scriptural suggestion, according to his sin. After that his scholarship was unexcelled and his conduct irreproachable.

Another severe test soon came to me. There was a tall, muscular fellow, seventeen years old, who made a dismal failure on a certain day. He was commanded to stay in at recess and study. A heavy frown gathered but he said nothing. When the noon hour came he ate his lunch, picked up his books and started for the door. " Where are you going, Jim? " I asked. " Home! " he muttered. " If you do go," was my reply, " remember that you cannot come to school to me again." He made no answer and went out.

The next morning Jim was in his seat with head bent low over his books. After calling the school to order the incident of the previous day in connection with Jim was related and the case taken up. Turning to the offender I said sternly, " Take your books, sir, and go home! " The boy's head sank lower and lower. There was a profound silence. Looking up finally in an abject, pleading fashion he said: " Miss Belle, please forgive me for acting so bad yesterday. I'm truly sorry. If you'll let me stay I promise never to disobey you again." The *amende honorable* was accepted, peace reigned and the spirit of insurrection was quelled forever. Jim was ever after my loyal vassal, helping me to dismount on rainy mornings and the first in the afternoons to bring my horse to the stump which was my stepping-block to reach the saddle, meekly handing my whip as the reins were gathered for the homeward gallop.

I became Argus-eyed and learned to control my pupils by sheer will-power. A rebuke was seldom given, a scolding never. They were simply *looked at.* The highest class moved along steadily; when it was finally surrendered, at the close of my régime, it would have been entitled to enter the Sophomore class in a college. Coming in contact with such rough specimens of humanity and expending so much energy in the effort to control them, told heavily upon my nervous system. Every afternoon, on returning home, during my earlier experiences, my first thought was to seek the privacy

of my room. Falling upon the bed in exhaustion my
pent-up emotions found vent in a passion of tears. I
had always regarded crying as an evidence of weakness
and when quite a girl determined that no one should
ever doubt my strong-mindedness; so, on going to the
supper-table, my appearance would be freshened up and
my face wreathed with the blandest of smiles. I studied
until midnight regularly to keep ahead of my pupils;
mastering books taken up by them that had not been
taught me in my school days, and applying myself
closely to mathematics which I had unwisely neglected
while at the Academy, for history, rhetoric, philosophy,
English literature and kindred branches.

For four years in heat and dust, in rain and mud I
trudged to that little school-house by the roadside. I
drank from the neighboring creek when the cistern was
dry or filled with debris, in either of which conditions
it was usually found. On freezing days I crouched
over a cracked stove that radiated little heat, with the
snow drifting down upon my head through the defect-
ive roof. In the winter season I went again and again
to find the house empty, to come back home weary and
disgusted, with my little brother trotting by my side
sputtering indignantly because he had not been allowed
to stay at home " like other folkses childerns."

Sometimes mid-summer sessions would be taught to
accommodate the larger pupils who had to be in the
field until the crop was " laid by." The heat was almost
intolerable, the days seemed unending. The drowsy,
germ-laden, suffocating hours would be lived through
in dreariness and suffering : but, hard as it all was, noth-

ing would be taken in exchange for the self-knowledge and self-power that I gained in this struggle.

The money that was made during the first session was invested in a course of study in the Normal College, at Iuka, Mississippi. At the close of the term a visit was made to the Southern Chautauqua, at Monteagle, Tennessee. Portions of other vacations were spent in Canton taking private lessons in mathematics from my friend, Mrs. Amelia Drane, a teacher of wide experience and unusual ability. She was the only woman, at that time, who had graduated at Soule's Commercial College, in New Orleans.

In the afternoons, at the close of her school, she would stand with me at the blackboard or sit near me for hours giving the most patient instruction regardless of weariness or the hot, chalky atmosphere. When our engagement was ended and when, according to contract, the requisite amount of money was brought to remunerate her, the tears sprang to her eyes and laying her kindly, blessed hands in mine she cried: " My dear child, *do* you suppose I would accept a dollar from *you?* Some day, if it is ever needed, you may pay me, but not now." Only in eternity can this noble, unselfish friend realize what she did for me in helping to make smooth the paths which, at that time, stretched bare and stony through my struggling life. Such a deed as that is far above price; it can find a recompense only " in kind."

Some time after my experience in teaching was begun, a new railway brought into existence the little town of Flora, within four miles of father's plantation. I was invited to accept the position of assistant teacher

in the public school there; a male principal having already been installed. As the salaries were still dependent upon the number of pupils in attendance, my remuneration would not have been an inducement had not
a promise been made that it should be brought up to a
certain monthly sum by the patrons. Board was offered
in a pleasant family with the understanding that I
should every night supervise the study hours of the little
daughter.

The offer was accepted and the term finished without
a jar in the school-room. Going away from home to
board and playing the governess, after nightfall, was
a repugnant prospect; but my association with the
happy household was so agreeable and my small pupil
so gentle and studious that the dread faded away, and
a friendship which has suffered no change in the passing years was the fortunate result.

The public school session closed in April—there were
only five months allowed by the law. I opened an independent private school in the Methodist church building. The principal of the public school occupied the
school-house. Three months were passed pleasantly.
The following fall another private school was taught
in Flora, which was conducted as easily as the first.
My only hardship was in having to buy all the wood that
was used and in making the fires. Finally, I was relieved of the latter through the goodness of a kind-
hearted patron.

Father was elected to the lower house of the legislature again and served in the session of 1880. In 1891
he was sent to the state senate. My oldest brother was

still in business in North Mississippi. My second brother had entered the Agricultural and Mechanical College, but, his health failing, in a few months he went to Texas for a dryer climate and sunnier fortunes. My third brother, after a course at a Business College, assumed complete management of the plantation, developing a decided talent for " turning a dollar."

Our financial affairs were now on a firmer basis but none of us had thought of relieving mother. While in the school-room, at Flora, one day the conviction suddenly seized me that she was ill. The impression grew with the hours. In the afternoon I mounted a horse and alone rode home to have my presentiment confirmed. In an agony of remorse I threw myself by the sick-bed and cried: " O, mother, please forgive me for all my thoughtlessness and selfishness! In these years since the way was opened for me to make money my only purpose has been to cultivate my mind, and it was forgotten that you were growing old, and now you have failed through work and care! "

A cook was hired before sunset and never since that sad day has the home been without one, nor without a woman to do the housework as well as servants for harder forms of labor.

CHAPTER IX

EDUCATIONAL MATTERS

If you would not cease to love mankind,
You must not cease to do them good.
—MARIE ESCHENBACH.

By degrees the public school won its way to favor in the South. It triumphed " over prejudice, over poverty, over opposition engendered by a large negro population which pays little tax and whose schools are a heavy burden upon the property owners." In the years immediately following the re-establishment of the " free school," after the civil war, it was considered scarcely respectable to patronize it, and the person who undertook to teach one was brave indeed.

To-day there is no position more highly honorable than that of a public school teacher. This revolution has been the blossoming of thirty-two years of budding sentiment,—from 1868 to 1900. For fifteen years the system was at low tide in Mississippi. In 1886 a complete change was made in the school law by the legislature. Teachers were required to stand rigid examinations before certificates would be issued. Superintendents were ordered to apportion salaries according to the grade credential held, the executive capacity of the teacher, and, though not dependent as formerly

84

on the number of pupils in attendance, the size of the school was taken into consideration. Payments were made promptly at the end of each month and new life was infused into methods.

The benefits of the Peabody educational fund were restored to Mississippi in 1893; institutes were held and in 1896, five summer normals were established for the white and an equal number for the black people. The moneys for the support of the public schools in each of the years 1898-99 amounted to $950,000, including the poll-tax, which is $2.00 per head. If there is a deficit in the school fund the state treasury supplements it. When needed, special local taxes can be levied by the district; also by the Board of Supervisors for continuing the school year longer than the uniform term.

The legislature, which met in the winter of 1900, appropriated one million dollars to common schools for the year 1900; also for 1901. Appropriations to the state colleges were very liberal. All of this, added to local taxation for extending terms, etc., will run the public expenditure to $2,000,000 for each year.

The school fund has steadily increased notwithstanding disastrous agricultural conditions and the facts that the census of 1894 showed that there were 100,000 more negro children in Mississippi than white. During the scholastic year of 1896-97, 367,579 pupils were enrolled in the public schools; of that number 170,811 were white and 196,768 were negroes,—the latter being in excess of the whites 25,957. The sum set apart for the support of the schools is prorated among the educable children of the state irrespective of color.

The proportional number of negro tax-payers in Mississippi is pitiably small; consequently, some idea can be easily gained of the relative amount of taxes paid by the white people for the support of colored schools. It is difficult to determine what is the best policy to pursue in the distribution of the school fund, as the races are very unevenly distributed over the state. The negroes are massed in the productive districts—the Delta, the river counties where planting is conducted as extensively as in ante-bellum days. By a strange misadjustment, according to the Constitution, in those counties where the negro population so heavily preponderates, third grade teachers receive higher pay than first grade instructors in the counties where the white people are in excess. From the report of a State Superintendent of Education the following facts are quoted: " In the white counties the whites are three-fourths of the population ; in the black counties the whites are one-fifth of the population.

" The ten white counties received $87,226 from the state distribution.   Of this sum they paid in polls $30,166, or 38 per cent of the whole.

" The ten black counties received from the state distribution $170,353, of which they paid in polls $32,459, or only 19 per cent of the whole. The white counties paid practically the same amount in polls as the black counties, while the black counties received nearly twice as much from the state distribution."

In the Superintendent's report of 1891-93, for Mississippi, it was declared: " It is a matter of common assertion by the uninformed throughout the state that the negroes attend school better than the whites. The statistics for 1892-93 show that 73 whites in every 100 of school age were enrolled in our public schools, while less than 60 in every 100 negroes were enrolled. The enrollment of both races was 64.8 per cent of all the educable children. This is a remarkable enrollment when we consider that the legal school age in Mississippi covers 16 years, from 5 to 21.

" According to the report of the Commissioner of Education (1889-90) Kansas in 1890 enrolled 27.98 in every 100 population, which was the highest percentage in the United States, the average being 20.27. The enrollment of Mississippi for 1892-'93 was 25.97 in every 100 population which places us second in the Union when both races are considered.

" But our enrollment of whites was 28.61 in every 100 of white population, which is greater than the enrollment of Kansas in 1890 by 63 in every 3,000 of the population. It is thus shown that our white population, as measured by enrollment, are availing themselves of the educational advantages provided by the state to a greater extent than the people of any state in the Union."

In the same report it was stated that Mississippi " led among the Southern states and is ranked eight among the states in the Union in the amount expended for education in proportion to the valuation of property." The State Superintendent of Education for Alabama makes this statement: " Alabama expends annually for her schools and education more than one million dollars; while her taxes amount scarcely to two millions.". . . .

It is said: " The state of New York has an assessed valuation greater than all the thirteen Southern states combined (Missouri not included), while New England and the Middle States together, with an area only two-ninths as large as the thirteen Southern states, and with a population about equal have three times as much assessed property.

" It is apparent, therefore, that with equal levies these wealthier states can maintain schools for ten months in the year, while in the South the length of the term will not average four months."

In all comparative statistics between the North and the South on the subject of education, or any other, it is well to remember the sparseness of population in the Southern states. For instance, in the city of New York alone there are 1,515,301 inhabitants! while in the entire state of Mississippi there are but 1,289,600 persons; there are but three cities of 10,000 or over, and but two others, with a population over 5,000.

In a paper entitled, " What the South Is Doing for Education and What Education Is Doing for the South," read by Dr. W. T. Harris, U. S. Commissioner of Education, in Atlanta, Georgia, October 26, 1895, the progress of education was briefly and interestingly summed up as follows:

" In the past twenty years the South has increased fifty-four per cent in population, but its school attendance has increased 130 per cent; that is to say, more than twice as fast as the population. This means that there is a larger proportion of the population kept in school during the year; while in 1874 an average of 14½ out of every hundred were enrolled in school, ten years later (1884) the average had risen to $18\frac{3}{4}$ per hundred, and in 1894, or twenty years later, the number enrolled is twenty-two in the hundred. Of all the people of the South, white and black, one in five is in attendance on school for some portion of the year. This is a large proportion of the people to be in school. Even in Saxony, which excels all countries of Europe in its school enrollment, the per centum in school is only twenty.

"Even after making allowance for the fact that the South has a larger proportion of children in its population than any other section of the Nation, this remains a wonderful showing for the wisdom of self-sacrifice of the Southern people. They are, indeed, building a ' New South ' and its corner-stone is the school."

CHAPTER X

According to the order of nature, men being equal, their common vocation is the profession of humanity.—ROUSSEAU.

AN effort was made to secure from the auditors and treasurers of the thirteen Southern states an official statement of the relative amounts of taxes paid by the whites and the negroes. Every state of whom the inquiry was made was heard from; but the information desired was unattainable as few keep a separate list of taxes paid by the two races. They concurred, however, in the following statement: " The great bulk of the public school fund in the South is derived from taxes paid by white people. Yet, that fund is distributed on a basis of population, so that the negro receives vastly more than his proportionate share. And the laws governing this taxation and distribution were voluntarily enacted by the Southern whites themselves."

The amount of property listed for taxation by the white citizens of North Carolina, as per returns for the year 1896, was $221,138,146; for the colored $8,516,353. The poll-taxes paid by the whites for the same year were $260,865.58; by the negroes, $100,-103.74. Taxes accruing from general property of whites, $399,554.48; from that of the blacks, $15,-

349.76. Taxes from polls and general property were given to the support of the public schools, but no discrimination was made as to the races.

The total enrollment of colored children in the public schools of South Carolina for 1898 was 150,787; there was spent on their education from state funds $204,383.30.

The white people of Arkansas in 1898 paid taxes to the amount of $2,621,538.31; the negroes, $132,111.20,—about one-twentieth of the whole tax—but no distinction of race was made in distribution of the school fund.

These instances, although probably very much more to the credit of the negroes' capacity for aiding in the support of the government than some other Southern states would show, are sufficient to illustrate what the South is doing to lift the colored race by education.

Very many poll-taxes of the negroes are paid in election years by white aspirants for office who want the colored vote.

The laws of each Southern state, while they provide for the education of every youth as nearly as possible, yet make distinct provisions for the establishment of separate schools for white and black children. Co-education of the races is not tolerated. It is an unwise friend of the negro who attempts to alter this custom. It is futile to advance a plea for the unreasonableness and unrighteousness of race prejudice. It is enough to say that it exists in the South and that it will persist there. It will not be disputed that the Anglo-Saxon and the African in America occupy the relation of superior and inferior races. The inappreciable number of the latter in the population of the Northern states precludes the question of social equality,—just as nobody thinks of it in connection with the Chinese scattered throughout the South. In some Southern states the negroes far out-number the whites, and are so numerous in all of them as to constitute what is called a " problem." Until the present generation they have always existed there as slaves. Nowhere on the earth have two races who bear or have borne the relation of master and slave existed together as social equals; nor do superior and inferior so co-exist anywhere until the superior is degraded to the level of the inferior. It is doubtful if there is nat-ural race prejudice; that is, if white and black children were reared together from the cradle as equals whether they would feel an antagonism of stock. Therefore, never will the South consent that its tender, unformed youth shall have the opportunity in the school-room to assimilate with an element that, in its present state, can only drag down the high ideals which the Anglo-Saxon has wrested from the centuries. •Better than any other the South knows that if slavery was an evil for the negro it was infinitely more a curse to the whites who owned the slaves. The blacks leave their deadly, im-moral trail wherever massed in large numbers.

This must be said, notwithstanding a most earnest desire for the advancement of the negro by education and all other wise means; and it is said with an old-time affection which is a redeeming legacy of the days of master and slave, which was a tie of love often stronger than blood, whose power a stranger cannot understand;

and which, alas! will be known no more when the remnants of ante-bellum days are gathered to their fathers.

There is a plantation in Mississippi where until recently five generations of the old slaves have dwelt as tenants upon the soil where most of them were born, and to which they clung with an attachment equal to that of the owners, and as much more pathetic as it was more helpless. " Old Handy " came into the library one winter afternoon a few years ago, to pay his " respec's " to his " white folks." " I'se pow'ful glad to see yo' lookin' so well, Marse William, I sho is!" " Yes, Handy, I am well, but I begin to think I'm getting aged. I've not realized it all along, but you and I have lived quite awhile, Handy!" " That's so, Marse William, an', please Gord, we'll live a pow'ful time yit. Yo' ain' broke a bit, suh, not a bit. How long's it ben, Marse William, sence yo' bought me?" " Fully fifty years; we were both almost boys then, Handy. You are older than I am, you know." " Do yo' 'member dat day yo' cum to look at dat batch o' ole marse' niggers what was put up to be sole?" " Oh, yes, I remember it well! It was the first time I ever bought a hand." " When yo' look at me as if yo' had sum intrus' in me, Marse Gillispie he say, 'Lor', Bill, yo' doan' want dat nigger; he'll neber do yer no good; he's dat fractious he's in de cane-brake near 'bout de bes' part o' his time.' Member dat, Marse William?" " Just the same as if it were yesterday." " An' den yo' kinder sarch me all ober wid yer eyes, an' at las' yo' say, ' He doan' look lak a bad nigger, I doan' b'lieve he'd run away ef he wur treated right." " Yes, and I bought you then and there!"

" An' I ain' neber run away, 'fore Gord, from dat day to dis! Is I, Marse William? " " No, no, Handy, you and I have had no trouble all these years,—and now we are old men, not boys any longer." " Folks talk 'bout hard times! *I* ain' neber seed no hard times sence I cum home wid yo' dat day. I'se had plenty ter eat, an' ter war, an' a house ober my haid an' good lan' ter wuk, an' good white folks to cyar fur me. I doan' know de meanin' o' hard times."

Not long after the plantation was shocked to hear that " Marse William " was sick, a thing they had never known to happen in all the long past. His present fac-totum, once his coachman, later his butler, brought a cot-mattress, and said firmly to the wife, " Miss Annie, I ain' gwine ter leave Marse William, day ner night, I'm *bleeged* to wait on him. We ain' neber hyeard o' his bein' sick in our lives. Tom, dat grown boy o' mine, 'ill sleep out in de hall ter keep up de fires." Two by two others volunteered to be within call in the library where they waited many nights.

Anxiety deepened and soon groups of old slaves were ever to be found in the hall down stairs waiting for the latest word from the sick-room; moaning out to " Miss Annie " or the doctor as they passed, " Doan' let Marse William die! Who'd take cyar o' us ef he went. We cyant gib him up! We ain' nebber knowed nobody else."

Faithful old George stayed day and night by the bed-side of pain, till he came out sobbing aloud one morning to tell the waiting crowds that " Marse William " had gone beyond the sound of their voices into the greater worlds where they could not follow yet. Then the heart of the plantation seemed to break. The oldest of the ex-slaves requested that they might be " Marse William's pall-bearers,"—and they were. The rest of them filled the galleries of the church from which he was buried, and in which for so many years he had been an elder; and to-day he is the highest ideal that life has brought to his ante-bellum servants. Those who are left are the most self-respecting and respected, as well as most efficient and faithful helpers on the plantation.

Let it be said here, and said with all the emphasis the fact involves, that none of the " outrages " which have so often disgraced the nation since the civil war are the deeds of the old slave, nor is the " vengeance " that of the old master and rarely that of his sons. It is the new element of both races that wars one on the other. This statement has been made of late many times, in many ways, by the Southern press. The following from a leading South Carolina journal fully expresses the sentiment of all in respect to the men engaged in the atrocity of lynching: " They represent Southern chivalry as little as the residents of the New York slums represent the Christian civilization of the North. Ravening mobs are not composed of gentlemen." The " Atlanta Constitution " had just said, in reference to that appalling lynching in Georgia, " Unless public opinion in the South begins to act in an unmistakable way, the lawless and ruffianly element which exists in all communities will make itself judge, jury and public executioner, and its victims may be innocent or guilty. It will only be necessary to suspect them of some crime. We shall have the courts abolished, and all classes of crime will be punished by the lawless element. Negroes will not be the only victims. Whites will fall under the ban of ruffianism, and we shall have such a state of things that civil war will be necessary to restore to the courts and to society their normal functions."

Another journal, in reference to the recent horrible occurrence in Kentucky says, " It is to the credit of the South that her public men and newspapers have been as earnest, if not as bitter, in their criticisms as have those of the North. Hardly a voice has been raised or a line written in condonation of the affair." The people representative of the best element throughout the South are strongly opposed to lynching and deeply deplore outbreaks of mob violence. They are urging as a remedial measure that as soon as possible after a crime is committed court shall meet, a jury be impanelled and inquiry be made into the charge. If an indictment is found that a short and fair trial shall be held immediately or as quickly as the ends of justice may require."

There is now and has been for a long time a feeling of insecurity in the South wherever there are many negroes. The ladies of a household—especially in rural districts—are seldom left alone day or night; and care is taken that they do not linger late upon the road when walking or driving in the afternoons or remain unprotected anywhere at any hour for any length of time. Southern women have perfect faith, however, in the power of the courts to protect them and believe that the prompt enforcement of law is the safeguard of any community.

That the punishment of crime by any other tribunal than the qualified and authorized one is a rapidly infectious and highly dangerous lawlessness, is proven by the fact that within the last decade there has scarcely been a state or territory in the Union which has not suffered from one or more of these atrocities. The question, therefore, is national in its bearings. Still, as the South has the bulk of the negro population, the burden of the responsibility for the negro problem, of which the lynching is but one phase, rests there, and sooner or later the Southern people will settle it in justice and righteousness.

The world is scarcely beginning to realize the enormity of the situation that faces the South in its grapple with the negro problem which was thrust upon it at the close of the civil war when 4,500,000 ex-slaves, illiterate and semi-barbarous, were enfranchised. Such a situation has no parallel in history. In forging a path out of the darkness there are no precedents to lead the way. All that has been and is being accomplished is pioneer states-craft. The South has struggled under its death-weight for over thirty years bravely and magnanimously. As an ex-governor of a Southern state has truly said: " The South has her ills, her sins and her crimes. What section has not? The South has had and will have violent shocks to her civilization. What section has not? The South has had her sorrows. God knows they have been grievous and hard to be endured. Whenever the South finds an ideal government without sin, a people perfect in law and perfect in its enforcement, the South will do its respectful obeisance and ask to be led into its broader civilization and its better power. Till then, and not till then, we shall stand abreast of all other sections, claiming as broad a civilization as any and challenging those without sin to cast the first stone at us."

"What shall be done with the negro?" far outweighs for the American people all questions of territorial expansion, for we have the African as a factor of our internal relations, our domestic policy and our every day life. It has been thought by some social scientists that a process of amalgamation would gradually absorb the negro.

There is no state in the South where legal miscegenation exists. Intermarriage is rendered void, the contracting parties are driven from a community and the minister who performs the ceremony is subjected to punishment. Besides, instinct and tradition oppose insurmountable barriers to such a solution.

As to the extent of illegal mixture of the races the following figures, from a reliable source, will afford some light: " Of the whole African population 728,099, in 1890, in the North Atlantic, North Central and Western states, 28 per cent were mulattoes. In the South Atlantic and the South central divisions at this time, there were 6,741,941 persons of African descent, of whom 13 per cent were mulattoes."

Another proposal has been the colonization of the negro in Africa and our newly acquired possessions. Left to himself, as in Hayti, the negro has always degenerated, and proved incapable of self-government. Whatever attempts have been made at colonization, as in Liberia, have been abortive. The negro himself is violently opposed to transportation; only the unsettled and thriftless want to go; and as has been said by a leading journal, " If 2,000 were sent out every week of the year, that number would simply equal their natural increase in this land."

Although the death rate among the negroes is great, as has been shown in a previous chapter, it is not probable that the problem will be solved by extinction. According to the last census there were almost twice as many in the United States as when the civil war closed.

Southern statesmen are trying disfranchisement of the colored men as a solution of the vexed question. The white people of the South are equally intolerant of the social equality and the political domination of the black man. Every device has been tried to prevent the power of his vote—from a shot-gun to a Constitutional amendment. By the latter method, in 1890, Mississippi, with an educational qualification, legally and peacefully ejected the masses of the negroes from politics. This initiative has been followed by South Carolina and by Louisiana. The South's representation in the national government is not thereby lessened, as it is based upon population and not upon voters.

This system has worked admirably, so far, in substituting a rule of intelligence for that of ignorance; it is worth the serious consideration of all states that have a large foreign population. Every year the movement to make the wishes of the rank and file supreme is gaining ground with the American people, as is evidenced by the growth of the initiative and referendum and by direct primaries. Only an intelligent suffragist is capable or worthy of so high a prerogative, and especially must he be educated in and imbued with the spirit of the American government. A large part of the foreign population that lands on our shores is less capable than the negro of American citizenship; it not only has no more education but must divest itself of previous predilections as to government.

If educational and property limitations of the franchise are not sufficient to ensure white supremacy at the South it could certainly be established by the following plan, submitted by Henry B. Blackwell, of Boston, Mass. He says, " The enactment of a law enabling women able to read and write to vote would at once so enlarge the political forces of intelligence and morality as to control the negro vote and the illiterate vote, absolutely, in every Southern state, as will be seen by the following figures taken from the United States census of 1880, the latest available ones for the purpose of comparison: In every Southern state but one there are more educated women than all the illiterate voters, white and black, native and foreign, combined. An overwhelming political preponderance of intelligence can be fairly and honestly attained at any time by the enfranchisement of the women who can read and write, ten out of eleven of whom are white women.

" By the last available census there were, on the present basis of universal male suffrage, in the Southern states and District of Columbia, 2,947,434 white voters, of whom 411,900 were unable to write, and 1,252,484 colored voters, of whom 951,444 were unable to write.

But in these states there were also 2,293,698 white women over 21 who could write, and 236,865 colored women who could write. If these two and a half million educated women were made voters, their votes would offset the entire illiterate voters, both black and white, who number, all told, only 1,363,344, which surplus, when added to the 2,836,574, educated male voters, would make an educated voting majority of over 4,000,000."

To my mind, the solution of the negro problem lies in the establishment of the home and in industrial education. The word home is as foreign to the negro's vocabulary as to the Frenchman's. As a rule the colored people dwell herded in their cabins, which usually consist of but one room. In this men, women and little children " live and move and have their being—" often most numerously. Remaining long in one location is a sort of intimation of slavery, so they change their quarters frequently. They, as yet, have acquired little sense of the dignity of ownership. Prosperity can attend no people who are indifferent to possessions, for this indicates a want of purpose, and a failure to grasp the fundamental principles of personal and public welfare.

There is, however, a more potential factor in the development of the home than the proprietorship of an abiding place, and that is the maintenance of the family life in unity and sanctity. Hon. James Brice has wisely said: " The family is the fundamental problem of civilization." The negro's condition will remain hopeless until he acquires higher moral ground. That is the secret of his destiny. This elevation will be effected through a truer concept of Christianity.   Stonewall Jackson said: " It is necessary to put the strong hand of the gospel under the ignorant African race to lift them up."   It is a matter of rejoicing that the negroes have built since the civil war 19,753 churches, costing over $20,000,000.   It is not the church that will redeem them, however, but the spirit of God in the church; the possession of a religion that will purify the life—at least from the grossest sins.   " The hope of the black race," Bishop Haygood thought, " lies mainly in the pulpit."

Industrial training, resulting in the power to produce, will lead to the ability to gain and retain property, and will thus become an agent for the acquisition and development of the home.   The two leading institutions in the South for the education of the negro are Hampton Normal and Agricultural College, at Hampton, Virginia, and Tuskegee Normal and Industrial Institute, at Tuskegee, Alabama.   The principal of the latter is Booker T. Washington, who was born a slave, but is now the most noted colored man in America, and the foremost educator and the leader of the 8,000,000 negroes of this country.   The institute at Tuskegee under his able and discreet management, has grown to vast proportions and its influence for good is broadly felt.

In the session of 1898 it enrolled 1,047 students; they came from twenty-four states and territories and from two foreign countries.   Work to the amount of $45,-288.10 has been done by the students while pursuing their course of study.   They cultivate 650 acres of land besides keeping in constant operation twenty-four other industries.   Graduates from this institution are now following almost every industrial and professional avocation. By giving to the world trained, self-supporting workmen Booker T Washington is doing much to solve the problem of his race. He says, very truthfully, " In our education of the black man so far, we have failed in a large degree to educate along the very line along which most of the colored people especially need help. . . . The fact is that 90 per cent of our people depend upon the common occupations for a living, and, outside of the cities, 85 per cent depend upon agriculture for support. Notwithstanding this our people have been educated since the war in everything else but the very things that most of them live by. . . . First-class training in agriculture, horticulture, dairying, stock raising, the mechanical arts and domestic economy, will make us intelligent producers, and not only help us contribute our proportion as tax-payers, but will result in retaining much money in the state that now goes outside for that which can be produced in the state. An institution that will give this training of the hand, along with the highest mental culture, will soon convince our people that their salvation is in the ownership of property, industrial and business development, rather than mere political agitation.

" The great problem now is, how to get the masses to the point where they can be sure of a comfortable living and be prepared to save a little something each year. This can be accompli;hed only by putting among the masses as fast as possible, strong, well-trained leaders in the industrial walks of life."

It has been said by an educator of colored youth, in

reference to ante-bellum days, that " There never was a peasantry better trained in agriculture peculiar to the South, and in the mechanical arts necessary to its successful operation, than the colored people.   Spinning, weaving, cutting and making garments, working in iron, wood and leather were parts of the industries of every plantation of any size." With the introduction of a new régime this form of education was supplanted by training in the classics and professions. To-day the young Southern negro, born since the war, en masse, is the most untrained, inefficient yeoman in existence in any civilized country.

In the slave states alone, it is said, the blacks have 281 normal schools, 238 universities and colleges and 270 institutions for secondary instruction. Yet all this education has not perceptibly advanced the moral status of the race.

It has been proven that the negro is able to grasp the higher education; but the number of those who seek it is small. On the testimony of teachers among the negroes it has been stated that only about six per cent out of the thousands who have been instructed in the great missionary schools in the South have seized the opportunity for advanced education. A negro has won prizes of distinction at Harvard; others have graduated from leading colleges and universities; a colored man has written a Greek grammar; an ex-slave of General Joe Davis, of Mississippi, graduated at Fisk University and at Oberlin and went as a missionary to Africa. He has helped to reduce a native language to writing, prepared a dictionary and grammar of it, and published a translation of much of the New Testament.

The president of a State Normal College in Mississippi for the negroes says he had a student who could read one hundred and twenty-five consecutive verses of Homer's Iliad without one mistake; but it was impossible for that same student to copy a figure in analytical geometry. To others who had mathematical gifts the languages were unattainable. Of course, these cases of unusual attainment are exceptional.

In a lecture given in Memphis, Tennessee, February, 1899, Judge James M. Greer presented a definition of the negro that will be endorsed by every Southerner who knew him, as the judge did, in ante-bellum days. The one generation since has not been long enough to materially change him, except as he has fluctuated in the chaos of his upheaval from slavery to the freedom to follow his undisciplined will and his disorganized circumstances. There will be much sympathy with these true and kindly words of Judge Greer: " I knew him so intimately in my own childhood, knew him as the trusted, loyal slave; knew him as my friend and my inferior, that I believe I may say to you that he was an anomaly in history and a contradiction in human nature. If he was wanting in settled purpose and determined mental effort, he was also without malicious hatred or puling complaint.   If he had the thoughtlessness of childhood, he had also its faith. If he was religious without reason, he was devout without hypocrisy. . . . If he was without fixed principles in his life, he was kind in his impulse. If he was without the knowledge of books, he had gained much from observation. If he never originated, he readily imitated. If his courage was small, his rebellions were few. If his family ties were weak and his domestic life fickle, his humor was great and his charity enormous. If he was uncertain in the line of *meum* and *tuum,* he was generous in distribution, hospitable in the extreme, and improvident always. If he was without profound wisdom, he was also without deep sorrow.

" I may say of him truthfully that he was a humorist without wit, a lover without constancy, a poet without words, a father without control, a husband without rights, a slave without hatred, a friend without equality, an inferior without resentment, a human without ambition, a man without a country. He became a soldier without discipline, a politician without statesmanship, and a freeman without ceasing to be a child."

CHAPTER XI

EVOLUTION OF SOUTHERN WOMEN

The only conclusive evidence of a man's sincerity is that he gives himself for a principle. Words, money, all things else are comparatively easy to give away; but when a man makes a gift of his daily life and practice, it is plain that the truth, whatever it may be, has taken possession of him.—LOWELL.

DURING the Southern Exposition in 1884, my second trip was made to New Orleans. The world had changed considerably to me since my first visit: my eyes had grown accustomed to larger visions. Since beginning to teach, every question that related to the attainments and possibilities of women was of intense interest to me; but especially her developed power of bread-winning.

Julia Ward Howe was lecturing in the city. She was the first woman I had ever heard speak before a public audience, except students on a school rostrum. Never can the eagerness be forgotten with which my feet hastened to the hall where she was to be heard, nor the absorption with which my listening ears drew in every word, nor the critical attention that was given to every detail of the speaker's appearance, from the lace cap that rested on her brainy head down to the toes of her common-sense boots.

She spoke on " Woman's Work." As she talked

brilliantly and fluently my enchantment grew. The remark that she had visited several foreign countries and
had addressed the women of each in their own tongue
particularly impressed me. How far away those
strange lands seemed! How wonderful to be looking
at a person who had really seen them! Going to Europe
had been the dream of my life, and here was a woman
who had actually been there! For many years an earnest desire had possessed me to behold a genuinely
strong-minded woman,—one of the truly advanced
type. Beautiful to realize, she stood before me! and in
a position the very acme of independence—upon a platform delivering a speech!

Since the development of my reasoning faculties I
had believed in the rights of women, although in an
article on that subject, written at the age of nineteen,
I had affirmed " that we do not ask for the ballot." It
would have been too shocking, and my radicalism at that
period was in the chrysalis state. There was born in
me a sense of the injustice that had always been heaped
upon my sex, and this consciousness created and sustained in me a constant and ever increasing rebellion.
The definite idea of the political emancipation of
woman, as a happy and logical solution of the vexed
question, did not present itself to me in a positive guise
until some time after my entrance upon the list of
wage-earners.

Mother and father had reared me in a very liberal
atmosphere concerning the intellectual and political
status of women, for they were both advocates of woman
suffrage; father was particularly ardent. He had often

said that it filled him with humiliation to think that his
wife and daughter were not his equals before the law;
and with indignation that the mother of his children
could be looked on in any other light.

It gives me deep joy to remember that later on in
our experience, on mother's sixty-seventh birthday, she
drove with me four miles through the country to attend
a suffrage meeting which I addressed. An Equal
Rights club was organized in which mother assisted.
Father, who was at that time seventy-one years of age,
was made its president. Another fact that I remember
gratefully is that it was my privilege to serve the Mississippi State Woman Suffrage Association for awhile
as its president.

Notwithstanding father's broad-minded position in
the earlier days it did not occur to him that *his* daughter
might desire to enter the field of active modern workers.
That was " the pinch;" but since my way had been
fought into public school teaching he had never opposed
my progressive views nor interfered with my under-
takings. By gradual stages he became alive to every
issue in which my interest was involved and did all in
his power to further my projects. He began to consult
my opinion on important affairs. Every family trouble,
every enterprise, every hope was discussed between us.
Perfect freedom of thought and expression had been allowed me since my birth, and absolute freedom of action
since my thirteenth year. The privilege had been
granted of selecting my own clothes and choosing my
own companions. After the beginning of my teens
father and mother never said to me, " You *shall* do this,"

or " You *shall not* do that." Since my clash of ideas
with father at nineteen, he has asked me at the beginning of each year: " Well, daughter, what are your
plans? " Often when he has been implored to direct
me on certain subjects or to criticize my actions he has
invariably said: " You must exercise your own judgment. I have perfect faith in your powers of discrimination." Mother endorsed these sentiments fervidly.

The freedom of my home environment was perfect,
but I recognized the fact that there were tremendous
limitations of my " personal liberty " outside the family
circle. An instance of it soon painfully impressed my
consciousness. Three of my brothers, the comrades of
my childhood, had become voting citizens. They were
manly and generous enough to sympathize with my
ballotless condition, but it was the source of many jokes
at my expense among them. On a certain election day
in November, they mounted their horses and started for
the polls. I stood watching them as they rode off in the
splendor of their youth and strength. I was full of
love and pride for them, but was feeling keenly the disgrace of being a disfranchised mortal, simply on account of having been born a woman,—and that by no
volition of my own. Surmising the storm that was
raging in my heart, my second brother—who was at
home from the West on a visit of over a year's duration
—looking at me, smiling and lifting his hat in mock
courtesy said: " Good morning, sister. You taught
us and trained us in the way we should go. You gave
us money from your hard earnings, and helped us to get
a start in the world. You are interested infinitely more

in good government and understand politics a thousand times better than we, but it is election day and we leave you at home with the idiots and Indians, incapables, paupers, lunatics, criminals and the other women that the authorities in this nation do not deem it proper to trust with the ballot; while we, lordly men, march to the polls and express our opinions in a way that counts."

There was the echo of a general laugh as they rode away. A salute was waved to them and a good-by smiled in return; but my lips were trembling and my eyes were dim with tears. For the first time the fact was apparent that a wide gulf stretched between my brothers and me; that there was a plane, called political equality, upon which we could not stand together. We had the same home, the same parents, the same faculties, the same general outlook. We had loved the same things and striven for the same ends and had been equals in all respects. *Now* I was set aside as inferior, inadequate for citizenship, not because of inferior quality or achievement but by an arbitrary discrimination that seemed as unjust as it was unwise. I too had to live under the laws; then why was it not equally my interest and privilege, to elect the officers who were to make and execute them? I was a human being and a citizen, and a self-supporting, producing citizen, yet my government took no cognizance of me except to set me aside with the unworthy and the incapable for whom the state was forced to provide.

That experience made me a woman suffragist, avowed and uncompromising. Deep down in my heart a vow was made that day that never should satisfaction come to me until by personal effort I had helped to put the ballot into the hands of woman. It became a mastering purpose of my life.

The women of the South have not sought work because they loved it; they have not gone before the public because it was desirable for themselves; they have not arrived at the wish for political equality with men simply by a process of reasoning; all this has been thrust upon them by a changed social and economic environment. It is the result of the evolution of events which was set in motion by the bombardment of Fort Sumter.

At the close of the war when the entire South was lying prostrate and bleeding; her fertile fields left bare and desolate, her lovely homes ravaged by fire and sword; her young men slaughtered or disabled; her commercial streams choked and stagnated; her system of labor utterly and forever destroyed; her social affiliations blasted and every feature of life dazed and revolutionized, the women of that unhappy time arose in the majesty of their hitherto undreamed-of strength and with forceful calmness and unmurmuring determination, put their hands figuratively and literally to the plow and have never faltered nor looked back. Their heroism has not been known as it deserves. When, after the war, the men were dying all about them from the hardships that they had endured in the field of battle, the mother-heart of the South said, " Somebody must live for the sake of our children "—and the women lived and worked. Those of the better classes had been accustomed to the control and management of servants and households, often of large planting interests. They were full of resources, and their naturally flexible temperament made readjustment easier to them than to men. For a decade or more, the boys usually went to work at the time they should have entered college, partly from necessity, partly because many of them had served in the Confederate army and preferred work to the confinement of a student's life. The daughters were sent to college; every sacrifice was made for this end, until, after fifteen years, the superiority of culture of the young woman over the average young man was very noticeable. Improving circumstances gradually corrected this inequality: but the tide had set toward the advancement of women in the educational and industrial field.

Now, over the South, boarding schools and academies with their meagre curriculum have been supplanted by industrial institutes and colleges where young women are drilled in common-sense pursuits that will fit them to be bread-winners; sending them out into the world with skilled hands and trained minds. Medical colleges once devoted wholly to men are now equally open to women. Among these is the State Medical College of South Carolina, at Charleston, Tulane University of New Orleans, Louisiana, and Johns Hopkins at Baltimore, Maryland. The following state institutions are co-educational: University of Alabama, Arkansas Industrial University, University of Mississippi, University of Missouri, University of North Carolina, University of Tennessee, University of Texas, West Virginia University, South Carolina College, Alabama Agricultural and Mechanical College, Mississippi Agricultural and Mechanical College; also for the negro race Delaware State College for Colored Students, Alcorn Agricultural and Mechanical College (Mississippi), and Agricultural and Mechanical College (North Carolina). Very much after the order of Harvard and Columbia, the doors of the University of Alabama have been opened to young women. The annex is named for Miss Julia Tutwiler, the noted Alabama educator, who has done more to secure the opportunities now granted the girls than any other woman in her state.

Four Southern states have industrial schools for white girls:—Alabama, Georgia, Mississippi and South Carolina. Mississippi was the first State in the Union to have a *State* Industrial College; also the first to have an Industrial College for Girls. There were industrial schools, but not as planned in Mississippi by the *State* for the *girls*.

Nearly all public normal schools in the South are co-educational. The custom is gaining in favor and there is a pronounced sentiment for allowing women to hold administrative situations in the educational system. In the field of instruction Southern women occupy an honored position. There are thousands of women teachers in the common schools of the South to-day, besides hundreds of college professors, principals of high schools, presidents of normals, county superintendents of education, school commissioners, members of school boards and committees on examination.

Two prominent women asked the State Superintendent of Education of Louisiana not long since what proportion of women were employed in the public schools of that state. He replied that there were about nineteen-twentieths. This is a fair average of women teachers in all the Southern states. Two-thirds of the 425,000 teachers now in the United States are women.

There were 1,391 more women teachers in the city of Baltimore, in December, 1896, than male teachers. It is a significant fact that the salaries of women teachers in nearly every Southern state, probably in all, are smaller than those of male teachers,—which fact may be stated as general for most states of the Union. Less pay for the same amount and character of work is a cause as potential in arousing the unrest of women as that they are taxed to support a government that denies them representation.

Hundreds of missionaries go out from among Southern women every few years into home and foreign mission fields and almost every group of worshipers, however small, has a woman's missionary society. The majority of churches welcome women to their pulpits and Southern women evangelists are counted with the most successful in the United States of either sex. Some denominations allow women to represent them in their local councils and send them as delegates to legislate in ecclesiastical assemblies. In the South, as everywhere, women constitute two-thirds of the membership of the young people's church societies. Young Southern women are beginning to ask for deaconesses' orders and although not allowed to expound the Scrip-

tures as ordained ministers, yet some have graduated
from schools of theology and many more are being prepared unconsciously to officiate as clergymen in the
splendid drills they are receiving in gospel training
schools, and the active work of the Young Woman's
Christian Association. Women are superintendents of
Sunday-schools, collecting stewards and elders, and are
filling almost every office known to the church except
that of pastor.

From early Colonial times women have conducted
newspapers in the South, written articles on strong-
minded subjects and produced many works of fiction;
but it was left to the women of these later days to blos-
som into full-fledged journalists, editors, reporters and
managers of great dailies, proprietors of magazines and
authors of books, forming a growing and brilliant host.

A young lady of New Orleans told me that she was
not allowed, several years ago, to go shopping on the
most elegant business street of that city without a chap-
erone; afterward she became a reporter for one of the
most influential papers, going out alone at all hours of
the day and night. This has been the experience of
many Southern girls. Numbers of women belong to
press associations in the South, and some are presidents
of these important bodies. Clubs, literary, industrial,
scientific and political, abound from one end of the
South to the other. Railroads are employing Southern
women as bookkeepers and telegraph operators, and
they are acceptably filling the responsible position of
freight and passenger agent. They are seen behind
counters as clerks, in drug stores as pharmacists, in of-

fices by the score as typewriters and stenographers. We find them successful merchants, hotel keepers, farmers and cattle ranchers, state librarians, cashiers of banks, postmasters, artists, sculptors, architects and musicians, presidents of banks, police matrons, trained nurses, superintendents of hospitals, instructors of gymnasiums, steamboat captains, and officials in the employ of our national government, supporting not only themselves but often large families. Southern women are rapidly entering the professions of law and medicine; many are promising amateur practitioners, while others have already reached the zenith of the expert.

When a man married a wealthy woman of the South, a few decades ago, all of her property passed into the hands of her husband. Mississippi claims the honor of being the first state in the Union to bestow the right upon married women of full control of their property. Since it took the initiative, in 1880, the measure has become popular, not only in the South, but in many other states.

When the bill giving women the control of their property was before the Mississippi legislature, its opponents argued against it on the ground that if passed and allowed to go into execution, it would disrupt families. This idea of the disruption of families has been a terror that has hounded the steps of the reformer for generations, but the home tie seems to remain unruffled, through all the revolutions.

Southern women have developed marvelously as lecturers and organizers in philanthropic movements. Nearly every state in the South can boast of women orators who have addressed hundreds of enthusiastic audiences and unflinchingly pushed their way through overwhelming difficulties to positions of influence and power.

Modern reformations have gained a foothold in the hearts and lives of Southern women that is astonishing to all who realize the intense conservatism that fettered them in other days.

The Woman's Christian Temperance Union was the golden key that unlocked the prison doors of pent-up possibilities. It was the generous liberator, the joyous iconoclast, the discoverer, the developer of Southern women. It, above all other forces, made it possible for women to occupy the advanced and continually advancing position they now hold; a position that is leading steadily to the highest pinnacle that can be reached in civil government, namely, the political emancipation of women. The hungry avidity with which the brainy, philosophical women of the South are taking hold of this great subject is something at which we cannot wonder. It is the natural outcome of their desperate struggles for individual freedom. This sentiment for woman suffrage is not confined to one sex, by any means. I have always maintained, and do now insist, that Southern men, as a rule, are stronger advocates for the enfranchisement of women than men in any other section of the United States except in certain portions of the West. The old-time element of chivalry, which constituted so largely the make-up of the Southern gentleman, has been handed down through the generations and now begins to crystalize in the direction of equality before the law for men and women. Southern people are hospitable to reforms, whether they come in the guise of religion, philanthropy or politics, if justice and righteousness lie at the foundation. The movement for woman suffrage has advanced slowly in the South, because very slight effort has been made there to secure the ballot for women, and the thought is somewhat a new one to the masses. For years, in different Southern states I have heard prominent men say: " If women want to vote, it is all right. We have no objection. As human beings, they are entitled to the same privileges as we are, and require the same legal protection. We do not give them the ballot because they do not seem to desire it. Just as soon as they demand it, they will get it."

When the constitutional convention was held in Mississippi, a few years since, suffrage came very near being granted to the women of that state; and in South Carolina, soon after, the bill introduced in the legislature for woman's enfranchisement was lost by a remarkably small vote in the senate. In 1898, the state of Louisiana, by constitutional enactment, gave to all tax-paying women the right to vote upon all questions submitted to the tax-payers.

There are several states in the South that give women the right of suffrage to a limited degree, and whenever they have exercised that privilege they have been treated with the utmost deference by the male citizens who met them on an equal footing at the polls. Kentucky enjoys the distinction of being the first state in the nation to grant suffrage in any form to women.

This was done as early as 1838. Of course, there are thousands of men in the South, as elsewhere, who are heavily coated with an impenetrable crust of prejudice concerning the hoary creed of " woman's sphere," who would oppose bitterly any effort made for her enfranchisement, just as they would fight any other progressive measure. To this class belong the liquor dealers, the wily politicians of the lower stamp, the ultra-conservative ecclesiastics, the superfine " swells " and men who have risen from the humbler walks of life deprived of early advantages of education and the refinements of elevated home environments.

Exactly as there are opponents among men, so are there thousands of women in the South who have arrayed themselves in a belligerent attitude toward the movement that was instituted especially for their well-being. There are multitudes of others who are still in a deep sleep regarding the necessity of having the ballot, and are continuing to drone the old song in their slumbers: " I have all the rights I want; " but there are many of their sisters who are beginning to rub their eyes and look up with a glad surprise upon the new day that is breaking, while scores of others have shattered every shackle that bound them to the old conditions and have walked out boldly into the flood-tide of the most benignant evolution that the centuries have brought to them, and are working with heart and brain on fire to materialize into legislation the most potential gift that civilization can bestow.

There are woman suffrage societies in every state in the South, and equal rights conventions are constantly

being held. There are women everlastingly busy in
sending out suffrage literature, lecturing and organizing political equality clubs, in supplying articles for the
press, in appearing before legislatures and committees
and interviewing representatives, in canvassing towns
and counties, and in every other way laboring to pro-
mulgate the divine doctrine of equality, realizing that
when men and women " shall know the truth, . .   the
truth shall make   them " free."

A striking illustration of what sort of energy and
persistence is in the Southern character is shown in the
efforts of a young woman who was born in South Carolina, and brought by her parents at the age of seven
to Mississippi, where she was reared on a farm near
Meridian. From her earliest years, she was possessed
of a great love for natural science, and was filled with
an ambition for a liberal education: but she was poor,
and the future looked shadowy and forbidding. It was
not so dark, however, as not to be overcome by a relent-
less energy. At one time her brother playfully gave
her the large sum of five cents. With this a yard of
calico was bought, out of which she manufactured a
sunbonnet and sold it for twenty-five cents. That
amount was invested in more calico, and a dress was
made and sold; then reinvestments followed till $12 was
realized. She persuaded her father to let her have an
acre of ground to cultivate for a year; her request was
granted, and from her own labor and the help of the
$12 a crop of sweet potatoes was raised which netted
$40. This amount just covered the required deposit
necessary to enter the Industrial Institute and College,

at Columbus, Mississippi.   Here she paid her board
for four years by doing dining-room work. In 1891 she
was graduated with the degree of B. A.

The next year was passed in Meridian studying medicine under one of the leading physicians. In the fall of
'92 she entered the Woman's Medical College of Penn-
sylvania, paying her way through that institution by
giving private lessons in physiology and chemistry to
the students, for which she received $2 an hour, and,
at odd times, working as a waitress in a restaurant.
During the summers she stayed in Philadelphia nurs-
ing, thus making her expenses and gaining much
practical knowledge. In 1895 she was graduated from
the Woman's Medical College, and returned at once to
Meridian. Very soon she was requested by two mission
boards to go to China and take charge of hospital work
there, but she said she felt called to practice medicine
in the South, in her own state and among her own people. Six months after her graduation as a physician,
she took the state medical examination and was granted
a license to practice—the first woman in Mississippi
who has gained such a distinction. Her reception by
the physicians of her state has been cordial and courteous. Dr. Rosa Wiss is now an honored and independent
physician with a success assured by the precedent
narrated.

The mighty principles that are now being wrought
out in the splendid lives of the women of this nation
received their impetus several years before the Civil
war. Jessie Cassidy in her compact little book called
" The Legal Status of Women," published in 1897 for

the National American Woman Suffrage Association, in the Political Science series, gives a concise but comprehensive history of the woman's movement in these words: " The first organized demand by women for political recognition was made in the United States in 1848, at the memorable Seneca Falls Convention. That suffrage should be included had not beforehand entered the minds of those who issued the call for the convention, but it was suggested during the preparation of the Declaration of Independence and incorporated in the list of grievances submitted by the committee. It came like a bombshell upon the unprepared convention, and after a long discussion was passed by only a bare majority. Lucretia Mott was one of those who at that time could not see her way to support it. The organization of different State Suffrage Associations followed, continuing the agitation. In 1869 Wyoming granted full political equality to women.

" Different degrees of school suffrage are now granted in twenty-two states and territories, partial suffrage for public improvements in three, municipal suffrage in one, and in Wyoming, Colorado, Utah and Idaho women vote for all officers, local, state and national, exactly as do men."

The following is a list of states and territories that have given the franchise in some form to women: Arizona and Oklahoma territories; Colorado, Connecticut, Delaware, Idaho, Illinois, Iowa, Kansas, Kentucky, Louisiana, Massachusetts, Michigan, Minnesota, Mississippi, Montana, Nebraska, New Hampshire, New Jersey, New York, North Dakota, Ohio, Oregon, South

Dakota, Utah, Vermont, Washington, Wisconsin, Wyoming.

In 1869, John Stuart Mill introduced the question of woman suffrage in Parliament.   This was the first movement that was made for it in England.   Since then women have been granted local franchise to a great extent and now a strong demand is being made for Parliamentary Suffrage.   The cause of equal rights is gaining constantly in many provinces and countries on the continent.   In a number of them local and school franchise has been given to women.   Full suffrage is enjoyed in the Isle of Man, New Zealand, and South and West Australia.   The following is a register of foreign countries that have given the ballot to women in some form: Australasia—Victoria, Queensland, Tasmania, New South Wales, New Zealand, South and West Australia; Canada—Ontario, Nova Scotia, Manitoba, New Brunswick, British Columbia; Cape of Good Hope, England, Guernsey, Ireland, Isle of Man, Scotland, Wales, Finland, Iceland, Norway, Sweden, Prussia, Russia, Austria, Brunswick, Croatia, Saxony, Schleswig-Holstein, Westphalia, Austria—Bohemia, Galicia, Lodomeria, Cracow, Moravia; Belgium, Italy, Luxembourg, Roumania.

CHAPTER XII

THE TRANSFORMATION

Why thus longing, thus forever sighing
For the far-off, unattainable and dim,—
While the beautiful, all around thee lying
Offers up its low, perpetual hymn?
—Harriet Winslow.

My last private school in Flora was continued only
a few months. At the beginning of the New Year,
1887, my pupils were turned over to the public school
and I sought a much needed rest in a visit to some relatives in St. Louis, Missouri, where six weeks were
spent. There was the usual round of society gaieties
but the extent of my participation was entertaining
numerous visitors, attending receptions and the theatre.

This breath from the old life found me as miserable
as five years before, full of the same restless and unhappy questioning, and more disgusted than ever with
the emptiness of an existence without a definite aim.
I was yearning continually for an intangible Something,
but believing in nothing.

On my return from St. Louis a lengthy visit was
made to Canton. My mathematical studies under Mrs.
Drane were resumed and examination taken, for the
second time, under the new school law, in both of which
first-grade certificates were obtained. My plans were

unsettled but wisdom pointed to a state of readiness for any emergency. Soon after going home a letter was received from Mrs. Drane inviting me to join her in the flourishing school she had established at Canton: "Not as my assistant," she wrote, "but as my partner; sharing equally my labor and my income." A short time previous father's health had begun to fail. This made it imperative for me to remain near him, so the tempting offer had to be declined.

In the fall, my fifth public school year was begun near home in a new school-house that had replaced the old hut—the scene of my former struggles. It was not necessary for me to go from house to house begging for pupils as in earlier days, but the same visitations were made because a great yearning over humanity had crept into my heart, and the desire of my life was to do something for its solace and its uplift. My eyes had slowly opened to many truths; among the chief was a recognition of my intensely selfish, inordinately proud and uselessly embittered spirit. I saw that there was poverty in the world infinitely more stringent and painful than mine; that there was suffering cruel and exquisite, to which my sorrows were as drops of rain to the fathomless ocean; that there was hunger for light and sympathy, the intensity and need of which I was but beginning to comprehend; that there was ignorance pitiful and paralyzing in the very air about me; that there was degradation within reach of my finger-tips terrible and communicable.

With the dawning of these realities there came the conviction that one and all ought to be remedied, and that I should be an instrument in a new dispensation. Accompanying this consciousness was the knowledge that my own shortcomings would have to be conquered before it would be possible for me to help others. Then began a closer self-analysis; my most prominent failings were singly the subjects of excision. I forced myself to think of others' wishes as superior to my own; my pride was humbled by every crucifying device that suggested itself. An effort was made to tear out all roots of bitterness and to cultivate every tender sentiment. Clothes were bought for the needy and journeys were made around the country for the purpose of soliciting food for the destitute. The sick were visited and the lives of those who sat in the shadow brightened. Books and periodicals were sent to persons who could not afford such luxuries and an earnest endeavor was instituted to soften their hard lots by sympathy with their leaden atmosphere and sunless prospects. Sins that were intolerably repugnant were overlooked and outcasts, in the darkness of shame, were sought out.

The wider the windows of my soul were opened the more distinctly was my true self revealed—odious in conceit, selfishness and prejudice. The greater my humiliation the stronger was my yearning for an infinite, inexplicable, divinely satisfying *Something*. At this stage of my spiritual awakening Robert Elsmere was read, Mrs. Humphrey Ward's famous book, which is said to have destroyed the faith of many. I was profoundly impressed with the difference in the life of Elsmere, before and after his renunciation of Christianity; so radiant and useful when in the fullness of belief, so gloomy and forceless when the light died out.

My brain began to wonder if such could have been the real experience of a human soul; if so, there surely must be a marvelous power in the possession of faith in Jesus Christ. Then came the remembrance of all the striking characters whose acquaintance had been made through books or personal contact, and they were carefully weighed in the scales of spiritual beliefs. It was found that the happiest and most useful professed a changeless faith in God, and the most objectless and miserable rejected Him. A desire grew to *know* that wonderful essence called religion which could effect such transformations and sustain such power in the human heart. " What is God? " was asked again, not impatiently this time, not imperatively, but with an undying hunger that all the years had not quieted. " O, my soul, *what* is God? "

In the solitude of my room the Bible was opened. It had been closed ever since the hour the knowledge came that my school-days were over,—soon after my fifteenth birthday. I began at " In the beginning " and read on through the Old Testament, finding nothing satisfying, but numerous inconsistencies, unaccountable incidents and mystifying statements. I laid the book down with deep disappointment. A feeling swept over me of utter repugnance. Acceptance of the story of creation was impossible; the history of Adam and Eve was considered an allegory. It appeared unbelievable that a man as cold-blooded as Abraham in driving Hagar from his home should be the " *friend* of God." Jacob, to my mind, was a shameless deceiver and a thief, and could never have been chosen as the father of his people by God. Moses was a murderer and could not have been divinely selected to lead the Hebrews out of Egypt and to " talk face to face " with God. There was no poetry in the Psalms because David wrote them, and the sins he had committed were so hideous as to shut him out forever from any suggestion of greatness or connection with the mercy of God. So it was on down to the last verse in the last chapter of Malachi.

A second darkness fell upon me. Heart-sick, my daily duties were faithfully done, but my difficulties and sufferings were not mentioned to a living being. The crisis was too sacred for the human touch. There are vast stretches of soul-land in the possession of every unconverted life where none but God have a right to tread. Silent and alone the fierce battle was fought to bring my mind into an attitude of acceptance of " the plan of salvation." There were no promptings of fear in my struggles for a thought of hell did not appeal to me. The pitiless restlessness swayed constantly in my soul. My intellect rebelled, my heart was as stone. The truth was no nearer my grasp than at first and my condition was as wretched and comfortless as when, without rudder or compass, my faith drifted out from me on the ocean of night, *ten years before.* Work in school and everywhere else was undertaken with more vehemence than ever, but my despair only deepened as the craving grew for a great Completeness. After many dreary weeks, the Bible was again opened and the reading continued where I had left off,—the first chapter of Matthew,—" The Book of the generation of Jesus Christ." What a strange, sweet thrill went through me! what did it mean? " Of Jesus Christ." Rapidly the pages were turned with eyes and heart aflame. " The old, old story " of the only perfect Man; lowly, yet kingly; gentle, but strong; tender and faithful— " the same yesterday, and to-day, and forever;" fearless in the denunciation of wrong, undismayed in the defence of righteousness, unconquerable in integrity, sublime in innocency, infinite in power and holiness; the perfection of humanity; the fulness of divinity!

As the reading went on God was revealed to me— translated in the life of Jesus Christ. What difference did it make now about Adam and Eve, Abraham, Jacob, Moses and David! *I had found Jesus Christ.* In the glory of that possession all unbelief vanished. With a triumphant, " My Lord and my God! " my soul passed into the liberty wherein He maketh free. O, wonderful revelation! O, divine consolation! O, perfect filling! My heart was " satisfied " for the awakening " in His likeness " had come. The hunger was gone. The unrest was stilled. The questioning answered. Peace, joyous and ineffable, that the world can neither give nor take away, swept through my being.

> " And I smiled to think God's sweetness
> Flowed around " my " incompleteness
> Round " my " restlessness His rest."

CHAPTER XIII

MISS FRANCES E. WILLARD

What power there is in an enthusiastic adherence to an ideal! What are hardships, contumely, slander, ridicule, persecution, toil, sickness, the feebleness of age, to a soul throbbing with an overmastering purpose?—MARSDEN.

FOR many years the conviction had more and more firmly settled upon my soul that a special mission in life would be my destiny. My highest ambition had been to be a writer. At an early age several short stories were written and, later, articles on education and kindred subjects were contributed to different newspapers. A talent for authorship did not develop satisfactorily, so nothing more pretentious in a literary line was attempted.

After my conversion the impression of being born for a specific work deepened into a certainty. With this consciousness came a definite act of consecration. All that was mine—brains, hands, feet, life itself—was given into the keeping of Christ to be used for His service. With this surrender there came from the fulness of a glad heart the cry: " ' Here am I. Lord, send *me.*'— *anywhere*—to the foreign mission field—to the slums of the great cities—to the self-renouncing vocation of a deaconess or to the isolated calling of a temperance worker—anywhere, O God! "

131

My school closed in April. A few days later father said to me: "It is announced in the papers that Miss Frances E. Willard, President of the National Woman's Christian Temperance Union, is to lecture in Jackson next week. I wish, daughter, that you would go to hear her. She is a woman of international reputation and is considered the greatest orator and foremost reformer of the day. You should make it a point to come into contact with such a beautiful character." "Oh! father," was my reply, "the weariness is so great after these months of teaching that not enough vitality is left to pack a valise!" The next day a letter was received from Bessie Fearn, in which she wrote, "Miss Willard, the famous temperance lecturer, will soon be in Jackson to deliver an address. Do come down to hear her and remain to visit me." "What a strange coincidence!" was my comment, but still I did not think of going. The third day after, a letter arrived from a relative in New Orleans, saying, "I shall be in Jackson next week and am anxious to meet you there. Please do not fail to come." "This is a very unusual conjunction of circumstances," I remarked to father. "Perhaps, after all, it would be better for me to change my mind and go."

The words, "Woman's Christian Temperance Union," had never fallen upon my ears until the week before Miss Willard came to Jackson, in 1889. Temperance lectures had been listened to from Francis Murphy and Luther Benson, and the Independent Order of Good Templars had been heard of, but I had never known of the existence of a temperance society composed entirely of women. Father and mother had reared me with the strictest ideas concerning total abstinence; they held most decided views on the subject. Mother had banished wine from her table before my birth, and had not allowed even an egg-nog at Christmas. The decanters and wine glasses were put high up and far away in the cavernous depths of the china-closet and the spiders had long used them to assist their constructive enterprises. The children had been taught that intemperance was more than a beastly vice and drinking, in any degree, a disgrace. When a little girl, attending a picnic, some gentleman offered me a glass of wine and a bottle from which to refill. This incensed me so thoroughly that glass and bottle were tossed into the muddy creek on whose banks we stood and I walked contemptuously away.

Uncle Kinch was more convivial in his tastes than father, and at his home wines and cordials were freely dispensed. By degrees my Nazarite teachings lost their force, the customs of the society about me were adopted and every sort of refreshment partaken of that was served,—wined ice-tea being a specialty. It often happened during visits to intimate friends that claret was " handed around " at intervals to the young people; at other times, while spending the day with a young lady acquaintance that the mother sent in a bottle of wine to be used at will as we played cards. I was accustomed in towns to see champagne flow at dinings, and I did not refuse it. Once a wine-party was given " to young ladies only " at which I was present. Our hostess had tasted the contents of different bottles before our ar-

rival. She soon become so visibly "under the influence" that she had to be taken to her room. Of course,
after that, she was "cut dead" by the "set." It is only
the sin that "finds you out" with which society reckons
seriously. At balls and parties I usually took champagne with the rest, but always in my heart there was
a sharp protest.

When the decision was reached that life held something better for me than a giddy round of butterfly flit-
tings, wine drinking was renounced with the other so-
called pleasures that go to make up "society." My
young men friends began to be talked to earnestly about
the dangers of drink and success was completely attained in making myself widely unpopular with the
fashionable ring. When the serious business of life
commenced there came a recognition of the dreadful
havoc drunkenness had made in the homes about me,
and the conclusion was reached that total abstinence,
and nothing short of it, was the only safe position for
any man or woman to occupy. The pledge was signed
but the temperance question did not take hold of me
with such absorption as to lead me to read on the subject; in fact articles bearing upon it had always been
skipped as very tiresome. Up to the moment of hearing
Miss Willard my interest in the temperance movement
was not greater than in any other religious or philanthropic enterprise. I was simply waiting on God, keeping my heart ready to obey any command and my eyes
open to catch the faintest gleam of "Kindly Light"
that should show the unmistakable way.

There was an immense audience present to greet Miss

Willard. It was afterward told me that she had visited
Jackson seven times before but had never been able to
secure a satisfactory hearing, except when she spoke, in
1882, before the legislature,—nobody else, however, being interested enough to attend. Mrs. Harriet B. Kells,
one of the brainiest, most cultured and advanced women
of the South, who had made her record as an educator,
and afterward became distinguished as a journalist and
leader of thought in the National Woman's Christian
Temperance Union,—had determined that Jackson
should hear Miss Willard this time, and, by the use of
wise methods, including elaborate advertising, had been
a potent cause of the assembling of the vast crowd that
sat and stood, anxiously awaiting the great speaker.
Many were turned from the door unable to gain entrance. The State Medical Association, which was in
session in Jackson, adjourned in honor of the occasion.

Seats very near the front were secured by my friends
and myself so that not a word of the orator should be
lost and not an expression of her countenance be missed,
in order that we might judge what manner of woman
she was. She came quietly into the pulpit, modestly at-
tired. The small bonnet which was worn she removed
before arising to speak. One glimpse of that face almost divine, one echo of that matchless voice, one
charmed moment under the witchery of that superb intellect were enough to form an epoch in a life, to create
a memory unmated forever. Miss Willard that night
was the peerless orator, the gracious Christian, the marvelous reformer who shall stand forth in history " until there shall be no more curse " and " the kingdoms

of this world are become the kingdoms of our Lord, and of His Christ." While she was speaking a vision arose before me of the glad day when not one woman only, but women of all lands shall have entered into the *human* heritage—as man's equal in society, church and state.

Mrs. Kells came to me at the close of the address and said: "You must be introduced to Miss Willard. I think she will like you," and drawing me forward to the altar where the speaker stood, presented me. A cordial greeting, an earnest hand-clasp,—then we passed on with the throng. It is a little remarkable that I had met Mrs. Kells but once before, and during our brief acquaintance there had been only a very short conversation.

The day following Miss Willard's lecture, in company with Bessie Fearn, a call was made upon a mutual friend, Miss Sue Tarpley, who was visiting in Jackson. When I was sixteen years of age this delightful woman came to live at her plantation which was within six miles of my home. We soon became constant companions and for eleven years she was my closest friend, exerting a blessed influence on my life. She came just when she was most needed in my mental and spiritual struggles. Although of the world and worldly-wise she had kept herself "unspotted from the world;" was intellectual, exquisitely refined and of the loftiest religious nature. To use her own words in describing a friend. "She was like a breath of autumn flowers, the undertone in music and all things else that are sweet and unforgetable." Although my senior by several years, she took me into her "holy of holies" and we found ourselves to be peculiarly congenial.

While we talked together in Jackson this friend said suddenly, "I somehow feel that you must see Miss Willard and have a conversation with her. These progressive women are total strangers to the traditions of my life, for I am hopelessly of the old régime, but you are thoroughly interested in them. Please don't waste another moment on me, but go at once." We arose to do her bidding. When we reached the street Bessie said suddenly, "It will be useless to try to see Miss Willard at this hour; she is at dinner, and wouldn't have time afterward to receive a call, for she speaks this afternoon at three o'clock, and it is now 2:30. Let us go around to the church and wait until she comes. You may possibly have a chance to talk with her before the meeting opens."

While waiting for Miss Willard, Dr. W. C. Black sat near me. He was pastor of the First Methodist Church in Jackson and an old friend of my family, having once filled the pulpit at Vernon. He had since risen to distinction in the Methodist Episcopal Church, South, and had added to his reputation as a most invincible antagonist of the liquor traffic, and by the publication of his recent book, "Christian Womanhood," which fixed his place as a scholarly, broad-minded thinker. In course of conversation he was told of my late acceptance of Christ, of my entire consecration, and of my willingness to be sent to the missionary field, to enter the order of deaconesses or to go into the temperance work. These three forms of service had clung persistently in my thought ever since my conversion.

Miss Willard came and went without my having an opportunity for one word with her. There were a number of prominent Mississippi women present, en route to Crystal Springs, to attend the annual convention of the State Woman's Christian Temperance Union. Miss Willard left immediately after the service in company with them. I supposed we should never meet again. My disappointment was keen.

CHAPTER XIV

THE NEW CAREER

To each man's life there comes a time supreme;
One day, one night, one morning, or one noon,
One freighted hour, one moment opportune,
One rift through which divine fulfillments gleam,
One space when fate goes tiding with the stream.
—MARY A. TOWNSEND.

WHILE at the breakfast table two days after Miss Willard's visit to Jackson the servant announced that Dr. Black wished to see me in the parlor. On entering the room he greeted me with the following statement: " I went to Crystal Springs, the day after we had our conversation in the church, to look in upon the State Convention. While there I told several of the leaders what you had said in reference to entire consecration and willingness to enter the temperance work. Mrs. Mary E. Ervin, who was formerly president of the Mississippi Woman's Christian Temperance Union, clapped her hands and said: " Praise the Lord! For four years I have been praying for a young woman to be raised up in Mississippi to lead the young women's department of the work. I have been commissioned," continued Dr. Black, " by the foremost women of the convention to tell you that your expenses will be paid to Crystal Springs and that you will be entertained there if you

139

will go down to the convention. They wish you to come
at once. You have one hour in which to decide and to
catch the train. Will you go? "

When he had finished speaking there swept through
my mind, like a lightning flash, as is said to occur to
the drowning, the memory of my past life. Scene after
scene in vivid panorama glided by. Then the thought
presented itself of what the result might be if this
strange call should be accepted. It would lead me out
of the trend of my old existence. Doubtless it would
mean renunciation of home life, the estrangement of
friends, the criticism of an unsympathetic world; but
through all my retrospections and forecasts there was
sounding a voice more than human, with an imperative,
unmistakable ring: *" Go! You must not fail to go! "*
The hour of my destiny had come. " My soul was not
disobedient unto the heavenly vision." The answer was
given calmly and instantly: " Dr. Black, in one hour
I shall be on the train."

Hurriedly my dress was changed, the street car
reached, my ticket bought and I was seated in an express that faced south. From the window a good-bye
was waved to Bessie. As the engine pulled out she
called: " Now, remember, Belle, you must return
this afternoon for we have an engagement to tea at a
charming home! " " O, that shall not be forgotten,"
was sent back in reply. " Meet me at the depot at four
o'clock." At the end of an hour or two, accompanied by
a minister, who came down in the car with me, I went
to the hall where the convention was in session at Crystal Springs.

What a novel spectacle it was to me! The delegates were massed together in perfect order, each looking so serious and intent; the stage was filled with women and decorated with flowers, while the walls were bright with banners. There were stirring debates and tactful engineering of parliamentary points. A beautiful Christian spirit, holy enthusiasm and sublime devotion for a great cause seemed to animate all.

A seat was taken on entering in the rear of the room, but in a few minutes Mrs. Kells saw me and sent a page to conduct me to the platform. There were Miss Willard and Miss Anna Gordon, the noble young woman who had accompanied the former in all her labors and travels and who superintended the juvenile temperance work of the nation; Mrs. Mary McGehee Snell, now Mrs. Hall, who afterward became the most celebrated woman evangelist in the South; Mrs. Lavinia S. Mount, the devoted state president of the Mississippi Union, and other distinguished women.

After the adjournment of the morning session Mrs. Kells said to me: " Now, my dear, if you wish to learn something about the Woman's Christian Temperance Union you must not think of leaving here before the convention closes."

" O, but I have an engagement for tea this evening in Jackson! " was my protest.

" This occasion is decidedly more important than a tea," she answered. " Send a telegram at once saying you will not return."

The message was sent and on the days and nights following I attended every session of the convention,

and was profoundly interested in them.   Miss Gordon's
address was the first I had heard given to children.   It
made a lasting impression as a model in its line.   Before
that experience practical illustration in public speaking
was an unknown art to me.

During a meeting, Mrs. Kells whispered in my ear,
" It would not be surprising if you were appointed state
superintendent and organizer of the L. T. L. and Y. W.
C. T. U."   The intimation dazed me.   Those letters
which slipped so glibly from her tongue were as cabal-
istic to me as the incantations of an Indian juggler. " Do
please explain all that," was my puzzled appeal.
" Why," she exclaimed, looking at me with astonishment, " L. T. L. stands for Loyal Temperance Legion,
which is a juvenile society, and Y. W. C. T. U. for
Young Woman's Christian Temperance Union.   It will
all come to you in the most natural manner.   You must
be introduced to the convention."

" Oh! don't do that ! " was my imploring answer.
" Being introduced to this body of women would be a
new and a terrible ordeal for me.   I should not know
whether to stand up or to sit down, to laugh or to cry."

" O, well," she assured me, " if you dread it like that
it shall not be done."

She forgot her promise.   On the last afternoon of
the convention, without giving me a hint of her purpose,
she walked to the edge of the rostrum and announced
my appointment by the executive committee as state
superintendent and organizer of those strange orders
with the mystical capitals.   " Will Miss Kearney come
to the platform? " she continued.   There was nothing

for me to do but to go. She took my hand, and introduced me to the delegates, who arose and gave the Chautauqua salute. In a low tone she said: " You must say something now."

" Impossible! " was my reply. " I haven't opened my lips before an audience since reading my Commencement essay, eleven years ago."

" Oh! but you must," she insisted; " this is a good time to begin." Turning complacently to the assembly she added: " I'm telling Miss Kearney that she might as well make her first speech here as elsewhere."

With a supreme effort I said: " Dear friends: I haven't a conception of what it means to be a state superintendent and organizer of the L. T. L. and Y. W. C. T. U. The existence of your organization was unknown to me three weeks ago. My ignorance concerning your methods is absolute; but something in my soul tells me that I must undertake this work. In accepting the position with which you honor me my promise is given to consecrate the best powers of my young womanhood to the cause to which this day my allegiance is declared."

Just as my little speech was finished Miss Willard stepped forward and putting her arm about me said some complimentary words of cheer. In a few minutes the convention adjourned and the women, old and young, crowded around, welcoming me to their sisterhood and extending hearty invitations to visit their localities, to speak and to organize. It was impossible to answer them. My voice was choked, my eyes were clouded with the mist of unshed tears. How strange it all seemed! What was to be the outcome? Not a soul explained my duties, not a suggestion was given. No one had talked with me about the Woman's Christian Temperance Union within the two weeks since I had learned of there being such an organization. I knew nothing of its history nor how to procure literature to enlighten me. In the rush of those few days at Crystal Springs no one had found time to answer questions. One morning I had sought an interview with Miss Willard at the home of her hostess. She walked up and down the parlor with hand clasped in mine talking lovingly and hopefully of my future, but it did not occur to me to ask her about books and papers bearing on the temperance question. As Anna Gordon had passed through the room she handed me a little package of leaflets.

On returning to Jackson from the convention, my next step was to go to Canton with the purpose of standing another examination in order to resume my school in the fall. I had given myself to the W. C. T. U. work, it is true, but it all seemed very vague; especially how I was to be fed and clothed, for the officers had told me there would be no fixed salary; I learned later that expenses and remuneration would depend on collections at my places of appointment. So the practical thing, it seemed to me, was to teach and supervise the work of the two departments now under my charge, not dreaming of going out into public life and making speeches. It presented itself as an absurdity that I should organize others into a temperance society in which my own name was yet to be enrolled.

However, my time-worn plan of keeping myself in a state of preparedness was available in this crisis.

I shut myself in my room and studied those leaflets that Miss Gordon had given me with the earnestness and devotion that final examination for university honors would demand.

On my knees, day and night, I cried out for guidance from Almighty God. No help could be obtained from my aunt and uncle, for their ignorance of the subject was as dense as my own. When their counsel was sought with reference to my going into the work, they both said: "Do it, honey, if you want to; it is a new departure to us; we can't say what is best."

In loneliness of spirit and yearning inexpressibly for some word of advice and sympathy, a visit was made to the Methodist pastor, the man under whose ministry my entrance into the church had been effected, when a little girl, and from whose hands had been taken my first communion; he it was also who had accompanied me from the train to the hall during the recent convention at Crystal Springs. In a very hurried manner he entered the sitting-room of the parsonage and, as hurriedly greeting me, announced that it was very near the hour for his prayer-meeting. While we talked he turned over the leaves of a hymn book searching for the needs of his coming service. "Pardon me," was my first hesitating venture, "but can you tell me anything about the Woman's Christian Temperance Union?"

"No, ma'am, I cannot;" still turning over the leaves.

"Well," swallowing to keep down a sob, "can you

tell me anything about the Washingtonian movement and the earlier efforts of temperance reformers?"

"Not a thing," bending his head lower to discern the numbers of his hymns. "Can you give me an account of Father Matthew's work in Ireland, or tell me if there is a Catholic temperance society in America?"

"I can give you nothing at all on those subjects," was the reply, leaning back in his chair and covering his mouth with the book to suppress a yawn.

"You, perhaps, know," was my last despairing effort, "of my appointment as state superintendent and organizer of the Loyal Temperance Legion and of the Young Woman's Christian Temperance Union at the convention just adjourned at Crystal Springs? What do you think of my entering the work?"

"You can do as you please, Miss Belle," he answered, rising. "Of course, you may be sure that you will meet with nothing but snubs. I should certainly hate to see *my* wife or daughter undertake such a life." He excused himself and went to his prayer-meeting—which was composed, as usual, of about ten women and two men—leaving me alone to work out my own salvation, or not, as might be.

My next thought was to go to my old friend, Mrs. Drane, who was a staunch Presbyterian, by the way, and unburden my soul to her. In her gentle, kindly fashion, she said: "I know nothing of the Woman's Christian Temperance Union, but from what you tell me about it and of your own convictions, I feel it is the call of God to you and that it would be spiritual suicide for you to disregard it. My advice is to go through no more examinations, think no more of teaching but give yourself wholly to this work for humanity."

As soon as my commission had been received I wrote to father and mother for their opinions. Mother answered: " My darling, I have always taught you to enter every open door if it led to wider service for the Lord Jesus. If you are persuaded that God wants you in this temperance work don't fail to enter upon it; and I will give you up if it breaks my heart. Flowers are kept in your room while you are away as before a shrine, and I long continually for a glimpse of your face; but my suffering and loneliness now are as ' nothing compared to the glory that shall be revealed in us ' through entire submission to the will of Him ' who loved us and gave Himself for us.' " Father wrote: " In a supreme moment, such as that which has come to you, no human being beside yourself can settle the question of destiny. It rests with you and your God. You are standing ' on holy ground.' I would not profane it by even a suggestion as to your duty. You are my only daughter, and I love you as I love my life; but if you feel divinely called to go from home to ' sow beside all waters,' I say *go* most gladly, and may the richest blessing of our heavenly Father attend you."

My brothers wrote later that they could not appreciate the motive which actuated me to relinquish a substantial salary as a teacher and go into a strange work without a dollar in view; but if my conscience prompted that it was my duty, they would offer no opposition but follow me in my travels with loyal hearts. All my fears vanished after receiving those letters from my dear ones, so full of faith and approbation. A renewed consecration of myself to God was made at once, promising to go wherever He directed and do whatever work He gave me and ask no questions about bread, but suffer want and persecution if need be to promote the blessed cause that claimed my fealty. Every association was rejected that hampered and every tie severed that bound me to the old existence. In the strength and majesty of a sublime purpose, I arose and shook myself free!

The call of God had come. Through that assurance a deep peace abided with me, a joyous rest in Him. There has been ever since a new song in my heart, a new light in my soul, a new inspiration in my life, a definite, sacred purpose that has never died out. My mission was found. No more advice was asked for, no more sympathy sought. *I closed the door to all the world but God,*—AND WROTE MY SPEECHES.

CHAPTER XV

MY FIRST SPEECH

Ah, but a man's reach should exceed his grasp,
Or what's a heaven for?
—ROBT. BROWNING.

AMONG the leaflets in Anna Gordon's package was one of Miss Willard's annual addresses and some of Mrs. Mary H. Hunt's publications on scientific temperance instruction. From these it was easy to gain a comprehensive idea of the scope and purpose of the woman's war against the liquor traffic and definite plans for the children's organization. On a tract designed for the Y. W. C. T. U., the name and address of Miss Mary McDowell, one of the national organizers of the Young Woman's work, were found. I communicated immediately with her explaining my ignorant but inquiring state and asking for some literature bearing directly on her subject. She promptly forwarded several leaflets. From this store of valuables sufficient information was culled to enable me to prepare two speeches,—one for young women, the other for children.

I had never taken an elocution lesson and knew nothing of voice culture. My unprospected field was entered literally without training. The state president urged me to go at once into the work of lecturing and organizing. She sent me the address of a young woman who was anxious to have a union formed among the girls at a little place near Port Gibson. While definite arrangements were being made for this trip, a visit was paid to my home for a greeting and good-bye to mother and father and the boys. Before leaving, a meeting was planned for the children and my first public address was given in the Baptist church at Flora. Notes were placed on a table conveniently near, but they had to be glanced at only once or twice. I talked without embarrassment. Several nights after, a meeting was held in the Methodist church for the people at large. No address was attempted but the manuscript of my speech for young women was read, and a Y. W. C. T. U. was formed. There were only four girls present, but every one joined. The smallness of the union caused many to smile. Noticing the amusement rippling over the audience, I said: " This is a weak beginning but I prophesy that within three years there will not be a saloon in this town." At the end of three years there was not a legalized dramshop in the entire district and public sentiment had been revolutionized respecting the liquor traffic.

A letter finally came from Miss Russell, the young woman near Port Gibson, saying that arrangements had been perfected and that she would meet me at the nearest railway station. One bright, hot day in June, about six weeks after receiving my commission from the Crystal Springs convention, I stepped off the train, with umbrella and traveling satchel, to fill my first appoint-

ment, as a W. C. T. U. organizer. There was no one
to greet me. On taking my bearings, the village was
found to consist of several small stores and a few residences scattered far apart. Nobody was at the depot
from whom information could be gleaned, it being
quickly deserted after the train had passed; so, one of
the stores was invaded and a clerk asked if he could
tell me where to find a boarding place. " Over the hill,"
he answered, jerking his thumb eastward. Summon-
ing my reserve forces, the climb up the dusty road was
begun.

" Over the hill," sure enough, there was a boarding
house, clean and white, close by the highway. On
knocking at the entrance, a tall, stout woman peered
from behind the door at the end of the front hall. " Good
morning!" I said cheerfully, her silence forcing me to
take the initiative. " Will you allow me to spend to-day
and to-morrow here?" It was Saturday; and I did not
travel on Sunday.

" Well, yes, I reckon so!" was the answer, but she
did not ask me to come in, and continued to eye me
cautiously. Still waiting, my interrogatives were plied
in self-defence. " Is Miss Russell in town?"

" No, indeed! she lives several miles out in the country and has not been here for weeks."

My heart sank. " Do you know Miss Russell?"

" Yes, that I do!" A broad smile broke over the landlady's face. " She used to board here and teach school.
Do *you* know Miss Russell?" she asked in turn.

" No; but she has been inviting me to come here to
speak on temperance and organize a union among the

young women. She promised to meet me here to-day."

" Won't you sit down? " asked the landlady emerging from behind the door, and apologizing for her lame foot and disheveled appearance. " Miss Russell may come in yet. I haven't heard a word about the meeting. When did you expect to speak? "

" To-morrow night. Miss Russell was to arrange everything."

" Well, nothing has been done that I know of. Folks are here from all over the county to-day to a big picnic in the grove back of the house. They ain't thinking about temperance. You can see them gathering now."

Looking in the direction indicated there were seen some hundreds of persons coming into the woods and disporting themselves in true picnic fashion. An inspiration seized me. " Since the journey has been taken here, I certainly do not intend going away without holding a meeting," I declared. " If a number of notices are written will you have them put up all over the picnic grounds? "

" Of course I will! " the landlady rejoined. Forthwith, my satchel was opened and in a few moments the following arrestive words were scrawled in a mammoth hand: GREAT W. C. T. U. MEETING TO-MORROW NIGHT! A MISSISSIPPI WOMAN WILL SPEAK! COME! COME! COME!

My coadjutor remained true to her promise and the notices were posted. Miss Russell arrived early the next morning and satisfactorily explained her previous non-appearance. Arrangements had been made for me to speak in the village church; an announcement of the lecture was read from the pulpit at the eleven o'clock service. Sunday night the church was packed with people who had come from far and near to behold the novelty of a woman speaker. When the audience was viewed from my position at the altar my courage fell below zero. The blood seemed to freeze in my veins. The opening services seemed remarkably brief and the presiding minister was introducing me to the congregation. Not a word that he uttered was comprehended by my dazed faculties, but when he sat down the fact appeared that my hour had come. Holding to the communion table for support I said: " It will be impossible for me to speak to-night unless some young woman in the audience will first pray." Miss Russell had given me the names of several consecrated girls who had received fine spiritual training at the State Industrial Institute and College, so one of these was called on. Without hesitation the noble young woman responded.

When the prayer closed my address was begun and carried to the end with ease. The manuscript which was spread out before me was referred to but once. The transport of enthusiasm, the inexplicable fervor, the exquisite joy, the utter abandon that often comes to public speakers in appealing to the intellect and stirring the emotions of an audience descended upon me. It was forgotten whether the listeners were opposers or sympathizers. Nothing was remembered but that my speaking was for deepening and broadening the outlook for young womanhood and the ultimate redemption of mankind from the curse of drink and the blight of social

impurity.   It is worth the effort of a life-time to experience the divineness of such a touch.

From the hour of my speech in that little town until
this day,—which means the test of nearly eleven years
on the platform—a manuscript has not been referred to
but once and notes have been used only two or three
times.   I concluded that decidedly the best course to be
pursued was not to be hampered by the consciousness
that succor was near but throw myself completely on
my own resources and trust.   At the close of this my
first address to an adult audience my second Young
Woman's Christian Temperance Union was formed.

Several years after this experience, Miss Russell entered the work of the Woman's Christian Temperance
Union as state lecturer and organizer and it was my
pleasant privilege to arrange a meeting for her   From a
girlhood of heroic achievement she advanced to an en-
viable position as one of the foremost teachers of Mississippi, and from the school-room stepped easily upon
the platform.

CHAPTER XVI

"AWAY DOWN SOUTH IN DIXIE"

There is no road to success but through a clear, strong purpose. A purpose underlies character, culture, position, attainment of whatever sort.—T. T. MUNGER.

WHEN my public work began, acquaintance with the W. C. T. U. was so limited that it seemed impossible to speak those letters in the order in which they should come. I would nearly always say W. T. U. C. or W. T. C. U. until they were conned over and over again—W. C. T. U., W.—C.—T.—U.—like a child studying its lesson. My *all* was given to the Woman's Christian Temperance Union and its service was entered with the avowed determination to succeed, cost what it might of personal energy and sacrifice. It was felt that I was called to push the work and not for the work to push me.

When Mrs. Mount, the state president, failed to secure engagements for me in certain places, which sometimes happened, if the towns were in need of an organization my creative faculties were set to work to accomplish our purpose regardless of the obstinacy of the hindrances. Every available orthodox means was used. A letter was first written to the minister whose name had been given as a sympathizer with the temperance

155

movement, explaining my mission and requesting that
he secure me an audience, provide entertainment and allow a collection to be taken at the meeting, to defray
expenses. If a reply was received saying there was no
opening another preacher was written to, and so on, until the ministerial circle in the town was completed. If
all wrote that it was a hopeless undertaking, then letters
were sent to leading Christian women whose names had
been secured through the ministers. If these failed
then men and women outside the churches were appealed to; the destined place was always reached in the
end, and a union among the children or the young
women was invariably formed.

After being fairly started it was easy sailing for me
in Mississippi. The loveliest homes in the state stood
wide open with a warm welcome; the press was generous in its expression,—even the papers most conservative on the woman question and prohibition never once
publishing an unkind criticism; and the blessed ministers, with a few isolated exceptions, gave me the heartiest reception and most cordial co-operation. Without
them very little could have been effected. They offered
me the use of their churches and the hospitality of their
parsonages; they spent portions of their limited salaries
to advertise the meetings, **hireing** conveyances to drive
me long distances through the country to meet appointments and **accompanying** me from place to place on the
railroads to insure a successful attempt at organization.
They failed in nothing that was true and brotherly and
Christ-like. To them the deepest gratitude of my heart
is rendered faithfully and reverently.   It is amusing

to know some of the influences that operated to intro-
duce my work. The third effort at making a speech
was at the Methodist Camp-ground, on the Gulf of
Mexico, near the little village of Biloxi. While there,
a young girl about seventeen years of age, was introduced to me: she was very gay, very bright, and an
ardent Episcopalian. It was learned that she lived in
one of the adjacent towns, back from the coast, and that
the place was full of young ladies. On being asked
if she would arrange a meeting for me on her return
home, she replied that it was quite impossible. In the
afternoon of the same day she went with me to hear
Bishop Keener preach. Returning from the service, she
said suddenly: " I believe, after all, an audience can be
secured for you in my town. In an hour or two I shall
leave and will write you in the course of a few days
what the prospect is." Within a week I had received
an invitation to come, had gone, had organized a very
large Y. W. C. T. U., and had been royally entertained
in the home of the young girl's parents, who were elegant people. Just before leaving my little hostess said,
with a mischievous smile, " Did it ever occur to you
that my mind was changed very quickly that day you
asked me to secure you an audience here? " On ac-
knowledging that I had often wondered what was the
cause, she explained as follows: " When you first spoke
to me I was undecided whether the dress you wore was
sateen or China silk. If it had been sateen you would
not have been asked to this place; but during the prayer
after the Bishop's sermon I found it was China silk, and
at once concluded to have you come."

" It is not fine feathers that make fine birds," truly,
but it has been discovered to my sorrow for humanity,
that it is often fine clothes that gain a hearing for a
speaker in an unpopular cause.

Day by day valuable experience was being added
to my limited store. In a few months a visit was paid
to a little country place, near Natchez called Washington, one of the historic landmarks of Mississippi,—once
the territorial capital and the place where the first Constitutional Convention of the new state met, in 1817;
the old Methodist church in which it was held is still
standing. Here Aaron Burr was taken, in 1807, after
his capture, en route on his supposed treasonable ex-
pedition to Mexico, and here he gave bond to appear
before the Supreme Court of the Mississippi Territory.
Jefferson College, for the education of boys, was located
there in 1802. This venerable institution now opened
wide its hospitable doors to receive me.

The minister who had invited me said : " Your meeting is to be in the afternoon. No one will be present
except some old settlers. It will be best to talk to them
on Prohibition." At that time, my knowledge of the
methods employed in the abolition of the liquor traffic
went no farther than the principles involved in simple
total abstinence; but some points gotten up in my jour-
neyings on the legal side of the question were put together, and we went to the church expecting to find
about two dozen elderly ladies and gentlemen congregated; but not a soul was present, and as soon as we
arrived it had begun to rain. Just as the thought presented itself of suggesting to the minister and the two

friends who had accompanied us that we return, lo! the
doors opened and in marched about fifty students,
dressed in uniforms, ranging in age apparently from
fifteen to twenty-five, and calmly took their seats with
exact military precision.

Terror seized me. There were only two set speeches
in my repertoire: one was for girls and the other for
children; the facts that had been prepared for the " old
settlers " would answer no better.   What *was* to be
done? As soon as the students appeared the minister
sat down at the organ, without saying " By your leave,"
and proceeded to sing; then he prayed and immediately
after introduced me. It would have been far easier to
have faced a fire of musketry in the heat of battle than
the calm gaze of those placid young men.   There they
sat, still and solemn as the judges of the Areopagus, not
relieving the cruel tension by the faintest indication of
a smile or a frown. While standing before them the
wish uppermost in my heart was that the planks of the
old church floor would split and let me drop through
to some happier spot: but as the awful seconds went by
and no hope presented itself in that direction, or any
other, a brave front was assumed, and going on the
principle that " honesty is the best policy " the deplor-
able condition was revealed to them: " Boys, I have no
idea what to talk to you about this afternoon," was my
frank avowal. " Never before has an audience of young
men greeted me. Your august presence is overwhelming. Since entering the W. C. T. U. work, meetings
have been held for the public, it is true, but my speeches
were made for the benefit either of girls or children.

You do not belong to the first class, so my usual remarks in that line cannot be applied; consequently, the nearest approach to the fitness of things will be to speak to you as if you were little children."

At this the reserve of my auditors was broken and they laughed aloud and clapped their hands. Encouraged by this demonstration of approval, without further apology I made a talk on Scientific Temperance, telling them of the evil effects of alcohol and tobacco on the human system. They listened with absorbing interest throughout, and, at the close, gave the most tumultuous applause.

That night was spent at the college as the guest of the president's wife. While sitting in the parlor after supper a committee of young men waited on me with a request from the student body that an address be made to them in the chapel, saying that study hours had been postponed, by special favor of the president, until the meeting was concluded. The invitation staggered me. " Oh! boys! " was my reply in real distress and embarrassment," you were told all that I know in the church this afternoon; my supply is exhausted." " Come and tell us the same things over," they urged. " The students are so anxious to hear you once more. Several sent word that if you would speak to them again to-night they would sign the pledge against the use of liquor and tobacco." That inducement was too alluring to be resisted; so my opposition weakened and consent was given to hold a meeting.

As soon as the delegation disappeared to report the result of the interview and to gather the clans, my room was sought, and covering my face with my hands to shut out all distracting objects, my brain was ransacked for every fact and story that had ever been read or heard on the temperance question, and every deed of pluck and heroism was marshalled forth, from the Spartan boy with the fox in his bosom to the valorous deeds of the armies of Napoleon, and down to those of Robert E. Lee.

In the course of half an hour an escort of a goodly number came to conduct me to the chapel which was filled with students and professors. Then my first impromptu address was made. The effort was richly rewarded by securing the signature of nearly every student to the double pledge against the use of alcoholic stimulants and tobacco in any form. The next day Washington was left with a glad heart but a wiser head. Dwelling on the trying lesson that had been taught me by this new experience, I resolved never to leave home again on another campaign without being fortified for every emergency by a stack of speeches to appeal to every class—from babbling babes to scheming politicians.

From the moment of enlisting in the ranks of temperance reformers, work was done with unremitting zeal. The eternal principles of righteousness upon which the Woman's Christian Temperance Union was founded appealed to my highest convictions and commanded my unswerving loyalty.

"In December, 1873, under the inspiration of a temperance address delivered by Dr. Dio Lewis, of Boston, the women of Hillsboro, Washington Court

House, and other Ohio towns, were moved to concerted action against the saloon.   They gathered in the streets to pray, and marched two by two into saloons.   They besought the men who drank to cease to do so, and the men who sold to give up the business, and invited all to accept Christ.   In fifty days this whirlwind of the Lord had swept the liquor traffic out of two hundred and fifty towns and villages."

The outcome of this crusade which was so strongly characterized by the outpouring of the Holy Ghost was the Woman's Christian Temperance Union.   The first local society of that great organization was formed in Fredonia, N. Y., on December 15th, 1873.   In August, 1874, at Chautauqua, N. Y., a meeting was held " from which the call for permanent national organization was sent forth."   In Cleveland, Ohio, November 18th and 20th, 1874, the National Woman's Christian Temperance Union was organized.   It was incorporated March 1st, 1883, in Washington, D. C.   Its growth has been marvelous.   " It has fifty-four auxiliary State and five Territorial Unions, besides that of the District of Columbia and Hawaii, and is the largest society ever composed exclusively of women and conducted entirely by them.   It has been organized in every State and Territory of the nation, and locally in about ten thousand towns and cities.

" The lines of its work are: I. Organization.   II. Preventive.   III. Educational.   IV. Evangelistic.   V. Social.   VI. Legal.

" Besides these are: 1. The Affiliated Interests.   2. The Standing Committees.

" Under the six chief heads are grouped various departments, each one under the charge of a National Superintendent, as follows:

1. Young Woman's Work.
2. Work Among Foreign-Speaking People.
3. Loyal Temperance Legion Work.
4. Work Among Colored People.
5. Health and Heredity.
6. Scientific Temperance Instruction.
7. Physical Education.
8. Sunday School Work.
9. Temperance Literature.
10. Temperance and Labor.
11. Parliamentary Usage.
12. Press.
13. Presenting our Cause to Influential Bodies.
14. Anti-Narcotics.
15. Evangelistic.
16. Unfermented Wine.
17. Proportionate and Systematic Giving.
18. Non-alcoholic Medication.
19. Penal and Reformatory Work.
20. Work among Railway Employes.
21. Work among Soldiers and Sailors.
22. Work among Lumbermen.
23. Work among Miners.
24. Sabbath Observance.
25. Department of Mercy.
26. Purity.
27. Rescue Work.

28. Mothers' Meetings.
29. Purity in Literature and Art.
30. Parlor Meetings.
31. Flower Mission.
32. State and County Fairs.
33. Legislation.
34. Franchise.
35. Peace and Arbitration.
36. Kindergarten.
37. School Savings Banks.
38. Medal Contest Work.
39. Christian Citizenship.
40. W. C. T. U. Institutes."

The World's Woman's Christian Union " is composed of national unions, and was formed in November, 1883. It is organized in forty nations, with a total membership of about half a million."

The reformation of the drunkard and the banishment of the open saloon were the primary objects of the earlier endeavors of that devoted band of women known as the W. C. T. U.; upon these rocks they still stand, but their platform has " widened with the process of the suns " until the White Ribbon movement rests upon a foundation of plans and principles broad and generous enough for the establishment of a church, a state, or a nation. Its purpose now is to carry the philosophy of Jesus Christ into politics, to make a practical application of the laws of God to those of men; to cause morality to become the rock-bed of our national life and brotherhood the ozone of its atmosphere; to advance the welfare of women; to defend the childhood of the world, and to protect the home. The numerous departments of the Woman's Christian Temperance Union form a mosaic of many thousand colors. The colossal figures worked out are God in government; man as the exponent of righteousness in citizenship; woman in church and state as the daughter of God and the partner of her brother man. In the brilliant array of glorious possibilities for the human race that the organization has held forth, it was the splendid opportunity for broadening and illuminating the horizon of woman that most attracted me.

Within the first year of my ministry I traveled into almost every section of Mississippi and organized over one hundred unions among the young women and the juveniles, speaking to the children in the afternoons, to mixed audiences at night; holding business meetings in the mornings to discuss methods of work best calculated to forward the interests of the societies formed, and to appoint superintendents of the different departments adapted to start the union to move in easy channels. As a reward for my strenuous efforts the Woman's Christian Temperance Union sent me as delegate-at-large from the State to the National Convention, which met in Chicago in 1889. That was my first attendance upon a *national* convention. The large number of delegates present, the thousands of people who thronged to each session, the admirable executive power displayed by Miss Willard and other leaders, the thrilling debates on the floor, and the fine logic and eloquence that blazed in the numerous evening addresses was all a revelation to me. More practical knowledge was gained of the Woman's Christian Temperance Union during those few days spent in Chicago, and more was learned of human nature, than in all the personal experience acquired in months of field work.

Nothing but joy filled my heart over my first efforts for the young people of my native state. For a number of years there had been a profound unrest in the heart of the girlhood of the New South. Faint echoes of the secrets of a higher, stronger life, struggling consciousness of the necessity for more exalted action, whisperings of unborn possibilities suggested aspirations in directions that before had been only dimly outlined. The surging, aching, loving heart of womanhood began to throb and pulse with heavenly assurances of the right to do and to dare, striving to find a channel through which it could voice its longings. The Young Woman's Christian Temperance Union, that vast force, with its multiplied interests and varied, ever-widening scope of thought and accomplishment, that splendid factor which had arisen in our midst like a giant in its power, generating such light and sweetness over the already luminous fields of modern philanthropy, supplied the demands of the hour.

It has been a benediction to the girls of the South whose lives it has touched. A subtle, unseen spirit has taken hold of the finest faculties of their souls and stirred to action every holy impulse, producing changed beings. Indifference has been turned to enthusiasm; selfishness has been broadened into sympathy; unkindness has been swallowed up into an abounding charity; idle hands have reached out for employment; narrow minds have expanded and become glorified by the quickening, uplifting agency of love for humanity that has poured, like a divine radiance, into their slumberous lives and raised them up to God. In the few years since the Southern girls have donned the white ribbon and enlisted in the ranks of the Young Woman's Christian Temperance Union, in conjunction with the young women of the North, East and West, they have assisted in campaigns for constitutional amendments; secured signatures to the Polyglot Petition; supported rest cottages, lunch houses and headquarters for working girls; taken charge of mission meetings at night; sent singers to the hospitals; dispensed substantial charities through the medium of the Flower Mission in their visits to prisons, almshouses and the homes of the poor and distressed; distributed literature, studied the subject of physical culture and formed hygiene clubs; introduced text-books in the public schools teaching the effects of alcohol and tobacco upon the human system; established loan libraries, engaged in evangelistic, kindergarten, social purity, Sunday-school, juvenile and press work; labored among lumbermen, sailors, foreigners and the colored population; conducted Demorest Medal contests, held Gospel Temperance meetings and obtained thousands of signatures to the pledge. They are now supporting beds for young women in the Temperance Hospital at Chicago, and in the cities have established drinking fountains for man and beast. They are raising funds to aid in carrying on missionary temperance work in foreign fields; circulating petitions among the high schools and colleges against the use of wine and all alcoholic beverages at class suppers and alumni dinners; conducting parliamentary drills, prosecuting topical studies and discussions; giving receptions and entertainments in their parlors, besides holding public meetings of a high order to create sentiment for the temperance cause, and educate the people up to the idea of total abstinence and prohibition and gain the co-operation of young men. They are offering prizes of money to pupils who write the best essay on temperance, and several are going out into different states as organizers and lecturers, and one into foreign fields as a missionary.

The young women of New Orleans, who were members of the Y. W. C. T. U., for a long time supported a room in an institution for the destitute, near the Charity Hospital, where men and women could find a refuge, before entering the great world again to seek work and a shelter. The girls of Richmond, Virginia, one year, raised $600 which they expended in sustaining a retreat for the sick. The Y. W. C. T. U. of Asheville, North Carolina, in co-operation with the King's Daughters, established an admirable, uniform system of charity by which the poor of the city were clothed and fed. The young women of Mississippi have been potent factors in bringing temperance sentiment up to the high-water mark which the state now enjoys. All of this blessed service is simply a faint foregleam of the noble attainments and beautiful opportunities which the future holds for Southern girls. When they devote wholly their latent, unused powers to rid this drink-cursed Republic of its over-shadowing curse, then indeed, will be started a wave of helpfulness that will swell into a great

ocean for the temperance cause and for the evangeliza-
tion of the world whose shores will be bounded only by
eternity.

The most hopeful feature of the Young Woman's
Christian Temperance Union is the standard that the
girls have set up for the equal purity of both sexes. " A
white life for two," is their war-cry. The day will soon
go by when a young man, indulging in strong drink and
poisoning himself with nicotine, will have the assurance
to ask a girl, pure in heart and life, to link her destiny
with his. The day is fast coming when a young woman
will place too high an estimate upon herself to accept
the attentions of a young man given to dissipated
habits. The watchword that will be handed down the
lines and rung from the hill-tops of advancement will
be: Sobriety, or no husbands. The new law that is
being evolved out of the old chaos is that when the holiest of alliances is consummated, it will be upon a true
basis.

The most prominent figures in this era of the history
of the South are the young women; formed for all possibility, ready for every development, capable of every
achievement; strong, earnest, brainy, progressive, comprehensive! The light of the future is in their faces,
the shuttles of destiny are in their hands, the suggestive tread of their oncoming feet sounds ominously near.
They have adopted the creed of a new philosophy. The
non-entity of other times has vanished; in her stead has
come the energetic, up-to-date, gracious entity who is
getting hold of the springs of power through legislation;
who is turning the locks of the doors that have shut

her out from the sanctum-sanctorum of ecclesiastical polity; whose sweet voice is swelling into louder, deeper tones, and is singing out from pulpit and from platform the glad songs of freedom, of advancement, of human rights and privileges.

CHAPTER XVII

HOW " DE CAP'N COME THU "

What's brave, what's noble, let's do it after the high Roman fashion, and make death proud to take us.—SHAKSPEARE.

THE first invitation that was given me to speak out of the borders of Mississippi came from Mrs. Caroline E. Merrick, President of the Louisiana Woman's Christian Temperance Union, and afterward one of the foremost leaders of the suffrage movement in the South. She requested me to attend the State W. C. T. U. Convention which was to meet in New Orleans, and to deliver an address on the evening that would be given to the Young Woman's Branch. Consent was forwarded, but considerable misgiving was felt as to my capability to reach the standard demanded by a city audience. After my speech in New Orleans was made an invitation was extended to lecture and organize throughout the state. Very soon a work in Louisiana was begun that has continued, not only for successive months, but, at intervals, through successive years.

My experiences in that state alone would fill volumes. A way was made into nearly every nook and cranny; from the Red river district in the North to the blue waters of Berwick Bay in the South; from the cotton fields of the Mississippi to the timber-lands of Lake Charles; often riding twenty miles in a lumbering vehicle through the pine woods to reach an appointment, or puffing down streams in energetic tugs through chilling winds and surprising sand-bars; entertained in an humble cottage to-day or in a mansion to-morrow; eating fat bacon and cold potatoes on a lonely prairie, or feasting like the gods on the Atchafalaya and the Ouitchita; depressed with illness at Grand Cane or radiant at receptions from Monroe to the Crescent City. Ins and outs, ups and downs, arounds and abouts, but God in all and above all.

There is no country in the United States like Southern Louisiana. It is a land of languorous beauty, of poetry and romance. From New Orleans to the Texas line there is an unbroken stretch of territory; a broad, flat belt that has been utilized for rice and sugar plantations. Numerous rivers and bayous roll peacefully through it, adding exquisite touches to the scenery. Mammoth live oaks, draped in gray Spanish moss, line the sides of the streams, their branches almost meeting in the centre, forming shady arches. Sail boats with their white and crimson canvas, steamers, skiffs and numerous other craft float up and down the waters; over rich oyster beds, under an Italian sky; through zephyrs soft wth sunshine and heavy with the odor of orange blossoms; in the midst of a tropical growth of plants and flowers as rank as in Central America; past ever-changing scenes of dreamy loveliness that soothe the senses and stimulate the imagination.

The most famous of all the rivers and bayous are the

Atchafalaya and the Teche, which are connected with
the story of Evangeline. Nearly every planter claims
the tree under which Longfellow's heroine rested in that
memorable search for her lover; but at St. Martinville
the " Cajans "—who are the descendants of that little
band of Acadians who left Nova Scotia in 1755, expelled
by the English, to find a refuge in this delightful land—
say they have the original and only Evangeline oak.
These people still live in the primitive style of their
progenitors, and, like Mark Twain's man in the Azores,
" thank God and St. Peter they have no blasphemous
desire to know more than their fathers." In traveling
through this section, one would think he had suddenly
dropped down into southern France. Dark, foreign
faces are seen at every turn and the jabber of French
tongues fills the air. This is the region from which
Geo. W. Cable secured the material for his numerous
stories. Here are the quaintest old houses imaginable,
the first story of brick and the upper of frame work.
Age and conservatism and fossilized ideas and customs
seemingly laugh at reforms. The church of Rome holds
full sway. The women keep up the religion. At Ope-
lousas there is a convent of colored nuns. In the hol-
lows of the trees about the grounds images and cruci-
fixes are placed, before which the negro sisters bend the
knee.

In visiting the homes of the leading sugar planters in
southern Louisiana, one would never dream that the
civil war **is** over. On all sides there are unmistakable
evidences of wealth; elegant residences, horses and carriages, coachmen, dining-room servants, governesses and

housekeepers; in the fields, hundreds of negroes working under an overseer, whom they *call* " overseer," as in ante-bellum days. At sunrise, noon and sunset, the plantation bell rings and the laborers walk, or ride mules to their work, so many in numbers they look like battalions, particularly so as each man and woman is armed with a hoe, carried on the shoulder like a musket.

It is amazing to see how the woman suffrage question is growing in this quiet section. Opinions are expressed endorsing the movement that surprises the unexpectant listener. The women especially are having their eyes opened; particularly those who have been connected with W. C. T. U. work. They see that the solution of the drink problem lies to a great extent in woman's ballot; and, looking deeper, they find that the key to the whole situation. Not only in political and philanthropic circles have women been brought to realize their restrictions but in ecclesiastical as well.

Morgan City is a small town on Berwick Bay. A Methodist church was built there largely through the munificence of Capt. Pharr, a wealthy sugar planter. Very soon a Sunday-school was organized and Capt. Pharr was requested to act as superintendent. He refused. Other men were urged to accept the position, but they likewise refused. As a last resort, the minister asked Mrs. Pharr, the wife of the planter, to be superintendent of the Sunday-school. She accepted. The Bay lay between Mrs. Pharr's home and Morgan City, and every Sabbath she had to pay from $1.50 to $2.00 ferriage in crossing to and fro. There were a number of children in a little fishing village near, whom Mrs.

Pharr wanted to take over with her to Sunday-school and church, as there were none near them; but the expense of crossing the Bay was so great she found it impossible to do so. Finally, she went to her husband, and said: " Captain Pharr, I wish you would furnish me a boat in which to go over to Morgan City and take the children from Berwick." The Captain refused, saying that it would cost too much; besides, there was no one to pull the boat across the Bay, and a man would have to be hired at $1.00 a day to do it, and it would be too expensive all around. So Mrs. Pharr quietly bought a boat on credit, and paid for it in one month by charging passage during the week to the persons who crossed over on business. Captain Pharr was so pleased with his wife's skillful financial engineering that he hired the boatman, and everybody went over the Bay to Sunday-school free of charge.

For five years, Mrs. Pharr was superintendent of the Morgan City Sunday-school, and collecting steward of the Methodist church. At the end of that time, she was elected delegate by the quarterly conference to the district conference, which was held in a small adjoining town. She went. Bishop —— was in the chair. The report of the Morgan City work was called for. Mrs. Pharr arose to read what she (for she was the church) had done. Before she had time to open her lips, the Bishop said, " Madam, it is not constitutional for a woman to represent any church at a district conference." Mrs. Pharr sat down in silence.

Two more years rolled away. Mrs. Pharr continued to act as Sunday-school superintendent, and to collect the pastors' salaries, as steward of the Methodist church. The time for another district conference came around. Mrs. Pharr was again elected delegate by the quarterly conference. " What use is there in my going? " she protested. " I shall not be allowed to speak." The presiding elder who was present assured her that his influence would be sufficient to guarantee her a hearing, so Mrs. Pharr went. Again the report was called for from Morgan City and again Mrs. Pharr arose to her feet,—this time to speak of the work and not to read a report. The new presiding Bishop said : " My sister, you cannot say a word in this conference. You can write your report, and let a brother read it ; but a woman cannot be allowed to speak." Patience had ceased to be a virtue. Mrs. Pharr replied, in a spirited way, " If I, who have served the Methodist church for seven years as Sunday-school superintendent and collecting steward, am not permitted to report my work before this august body of men, no brother for me shall read what I have done. Bishop, don't you think you preachers are a little inconsistent? You urge the women of your church to crucify themselves constantly in class-meetings by giving their sacred personal experiences, and call on them to pray in public gatherings ; but after a woman has done all the work she can in the church, she is not permitted to tell of it." There was no reply. The presiding elder was asked to report the work done in the Morgan City church, and Mrs. Pharr went home the second time unheard, and quietly resumed the double office she had held for seven years, continuing to perform the duties incident without a murmur, until her husband accepted Christianity and came to her relief. This experience formed an epoch in her existence and made history that shall stand as a light-house for other women to steer by, and to which they shall look back smilingly in the better days that are coming.

When Capt. Pharr first moved to St. Mary's parish he was very irreligious. He owned a line of steamboats that ran up and down the Atchafalaya from New Iberia to New Orleans. Soon after his marriage his wife, who was very devout, said to him: "Sunday traffic is a terrible offense in the sight of God. You must stop your boats from running on the Sabbath." "What!" he exclaimed, in his stentorian voice that made the very rafters ring, "stop *my* boats when every other man's boats are running on Sunday! It would be sheer madness! It would ruin me forever!" "Capt. Pharr," she persisted, "I shall never use a cent that comes from the desecration of the Lord's Day, either for myself or my children. It would be preferable to suffer want than to roll in riches that came from such a source. If you will sell out your boats and go into some other business I will work to help you get another start."

The Captain rebelled fiercely for awhile, but finally concluded that nothing could withstand a determined woman, especially when backed by religious fervor. In a short while he disposed of every boat and invested the money in a sugar plantation. Fortune favored his new

venture and wealth poured into his hands. His possessions became great and his home on Berwick Bay is one
of the most magnificent in the entire South.

The story of Captain Pharr's conversion is exceedingly interesting. He had a way of rising very early
as he did in the days when he was a penniless boy in
North Carolina and of going about his premises attending to any work that required oversight. Mrs. Pharr
held family prayers with her three little sons every
morning before breakfast. The Captain returned from
his tour of inspection sooner than usual one day. As
he reached the door of the sitting-room his attention
was arrested by the sound of a childish voice in prayer.
His oldest son was saying, " Dear Lord Jesus, bless my
papa and make him a Christian." Then the second boy
began his prayer with " Our Father who art in heaven,"
and ended : " Dear Lord Jesus, bless my papa and make
him a Christian." The third little fellow repeated the
same prayer and finished with the same request that his
father be made a Christian. At last Mrs. Pharr prayed
most earnestly for the blessing of God to rest on her
family, returning thanks for all that had come to them
through the riches of His grace, and ended her petition
with, " O, God, open the eyes of my husband and bring
him to a full knowledge of Jesus Christ."   Captain
Pharr said it broke his heart. He made a complete surrender, then and there, to God. This was before he sold
his line of steamboats.

Once, while in Georgia, I heard an evangelist, who
had been entertained at Captain Pharr's home, tell the
story of the conversion of a certain steamboat captain

which was very similar to the experience of Captain Pharr, with the addition of an incident illustrative of its results. The revivalist said that the news spread among the hands on the boats that " de Cap'n had come thu." " Comin' thu " is an expression common with the negroes, implying that a profession of religion has been made; " thu " being a contraction of the word through. The phrase has originated from the custom that the colored people have of going into trances and making visits through heaven and hell, hearing " unspeakable words, which it is not lawful for a man to utter," before they declare themselves fit subjects for baptism. One of the boats was loading up for a trip to New Orleans. Everything was in a great stir. There were loud calls and impatient answers, perpetual runnings to and fro, and a general mixture of gay songs and muttered curses filled the air. Dinah, the stewardess, had finished her work and was standing calmly in the sun talking to the cook. " Aunt Milly," she asked with an awe-struck face, " did yo' know dat de Cap'n had done come thu? " " Hush, nigger! " said Aunt Milly, " doan' yo' talk sech fool'ry as dat ter me. De jedgmen' will be here 'fore de Cap'n come thu." " Sho's I live, Aunt Milly," exclaimed Dinah, " it's de Gord's truf! Hezekiah tole me he *seed* de Cap'n come thu one day while de missus was er prayin' wid de chilluns. Hezekiah's him what waits on de white folks' table,— Aunt Felicy Ann's boy, Hezekiah—him what lives nex' to us house whar de hopper-grasses am so powerful thick in de spring. *He* are de boy." " Go off, Dinah! I ain' los' *all* my gumption *yit!* 'Spec' I'se gwine ter

'blieve dat rascally chile, Hezekiah? When de Cap'n
come thu dis ere ole 'ooman's gwine straight home ter
Gabrell. Go 'way, nigger, I'se gwine *whar* I'se gwine!
Dat's whar I'se gwine. Take yo' brack se'f off!'"

At that moment the Captain walked out in full view
of them and said to the deck hands: " Now, boys, put
up the smoke-stack! We ought to have been five miles
down the river by this time." The negro men sprang
to obey orders and to adjust the smoke-stack, the upper
joint of which had just fallen. As they got it in place,
and the Captain was about to give the command for the
boat to " shove off," down it came rolling, missing the
Captain's head by half an inch, and scattering soot fore-
and-aft. The Captain opened his lips to swear as he
had been in the habit of doing all his life on such aggra-
vating occasions ; but his face grew suddenly very white
and the oaths died in his throat unuttered. With a most
heroic effort he summoned up a smile and said : " That
is all right, boys! Of course you couldn't help it. Now,
let's at it again!" Once more the men worked like
beavers and adjusted the joint. The bell began to give
the signal to " cut loose," when down lumbered the pipe
the second time, bringing a shower of cinders and a
shadow of dismay. The Captain's face grew red with
rage, and his eyes blazed ; but he checked the volume of
imprecations surging between his teeth, bit his lips and
walked rapidly to the stern of the boat and gazed down
the river. When he regained control of himself he returned, and cried out, " All right, boys! We'll try it
again!" Once more the men tugged and pulled and
screwed the smoke-stack in place. Surely it would stay

this time. The sun was high in the heavens. The time for starting was already two hours behind. The Captain paced up and down trying to suppress his impatience. The boat loosed from its moorings and began to puff down the Atchafalaya, when, lo! with a terrific thud the smoke-pipe fell the third time. Without moving a muscle of his face the Captain called out, " Come on, boys! that joint's down again. I'll help you put it up this time and if it falls any more I'll order a new one as soon as I get to New Orleans."

Afar off, and unseen, Dinah and Aunt Milly had been watching and listening with their hearts in their mouths. At the Captain's last words Aunt Milly clapped her hands to her head and exclaimed, " 'Fore de Lord, Dinah, de Cap'n's sho come thu! "

On visiting Captain Pharr's home after hearing the evangelist relate this incident I told it to him, and asked if it were not a chapter out of his own life. He was indignant, and exclaimed wrathfully, " The *idea* of my being such a poor steamboat man as to allow a smoke-stack to fall three times! If that absurdity was published to the world as connected with me it would ruin my reputation as a captain and the reputation of the story-teller for veracity. The negroes got their idea of my conversion from seeing me hoist a steamboat chimney one day and not lose my temper."

Whether in adjusting the smoke-stack or hoisting a chimney it matters not. One thing is very certain: " The Cap'n's sho come thu."

CHAPTER XVIII

A SOUTHERN PILGRIMAGE

The earnestness of life is the only passport to the satisfaction of life.—THEODORE PARKER.

Two years after entering the work of the Woman's Christian Temperance Union I was sent as a delegate from Mississippi to the National Convention which met in Boston, in 1891, and was there made a national organizer and lecturer for that association. The city was reached in time to allow me the privilege of attending the first international convention ever held by the white ribboners. There were women from almost every civilized country on the face of the earth, all coming together in one great work, all meeting on one broad platform, all having "one Lord, one faith, one baptism."

While in Boston a reception was given by the Massachusetts Woman Suffrage Association and the Woman Suffrage League of the city to the delegates of the National W. C. T. U. Convention, who were interested in the living question of the political emancipation of women. As it had been an engrossing faith with me for years, I gladly profited by the opportunity to become a part of such an historic occasion.

After an hour spent in social intercourse Lucy Stone, noble heroine, devoted apostle and dauntless pioneer of the Equal Rights movement of this country, called the meeting to order and requested that the guests make brief speeches regarding their convictions on the subject of Woman Suffrage, and stating the position it occupied in the estimation of the public in the sections where they lived. Mrs. Julia Ward Howe, who appeared before me for the first time since my early experience in New Orleans, welcomed the visitors. Prominent Southern women, among them Mrs. Lide Merriwether, of Tennessee, and Miss Frances Griffin of Alabama, expressed themselves as being entirely in sympathy with the cause of Equal Rights. The Northern and Western women who spoke afterward were not more radical. This meeting did much to bring into closer unity the leaders in the two greatest reforms of the nineteenth century—the Woman's Christian Temperance Union and the Woman Suffrage Association.

After the adjournment of the national convention I made Boston my headquarters for two weeks while visits were paid to its classic suburbs.

On my return to Mississippi, I stopped en route in Washington. The beautiful capital has since become the scene of many notable occasions in my life. The most prominent were the tremendous meeting held in Convention hall, which seated 7,000 people, in honor of the presentation of the Polyglot Petition, in 1895, to the President of the United States; the Woman's Council in the same year; the International Convention of the Christian Endeavor, in 1896, and the National Convention of the American Woman Suffrage Association, in 1898.

During the three years following I traveled through nearly every Southern state in the interest of the Woman's Christian Temperance Union, from Delaware to Texas, speaking in halls, parlors, churches, theatres, school-houses and in the open air; to negroes as well as to the white population; to audiences of children, young women, and mixed assemblies; in public and private schools, colleges and universities for both boys and girls; before conferences of ministers, chautauquas, schools of methods, State Teachers' Associations; State and National Conventions of the W. C. T. U., the Christian Endeavor, and Woman Suffrage Association, and have lobbied in the Mississippi legislature to secure the passage of the Scientific Temperance Instruction bill. The most interesting of all these tours was the visit to the Naval Academy at Annapolis, and to the home of the Southern novelist, Augusta Evans Wilson, in Mobile.

Often in small towns I have spent the entire morning in going from house to house telling the people of our work, and drumming up a congregation to hear me at night. At other times I have been met at the railway station by committees bearing flowers, and have been carried to handsome homes behind white horses, in a carriage decorated with white ribbons, to be welcomed later on by tremendous city audiences. Week by week I have lectured twice a day and have organized unions wherever there was the faintest possibility of success; and in almost every case have been received with cheering cordiality and treated with the utmost appreciation and generous hospitality. If there **is** strong prejudice in the hearts of the Southern people against woman's public work, as the world at large is inclined to believe, the force of it has never been felt by me. Opposition either subsided or was silent in the presence of my exuberant enthusiasm. Girls belonging to the most conservative and cultured families joined the Young Woman's Christian Temperance Union and developed into admirable philanthropists; gentle, timid ladies from the seclusion of their home life unhesitatingly entered the ranks of the mother society, and men, unused to the " new woman " movement smiled approval and gave their heartiest support.

The conviction has grown with my wider knowledge of them that Southerners, though tenacious of social traditions, are hospitable to new ideas and are chivalrous toward a woman who wishes their co-operation provided that she comes to them also as a lady. A study of state codes will show that the South has led in making women equal with men before the law. Owing partly to the simplicity of its social structure new thoughts permeate quickly; and being throughout a religious people moral questions, such as the temperance reform, if put to the popular white Southern vote would win by a large majority; and if the dangers of negro suffrage were settled forever it is scarcely a matter of doubt but that the men of the South would trust the women with the ballot, except in those states where there is a large illiterate white vote; and this, not only because ignorance is an insurmountable obstacle to progress, but because the unscrupulous politician is always on hand bidding for this vote.

That the above statement respecting the attitude of the South towards the temperance question is not extravagant may be inferred from the following facts furnished by chairmen of the executive committees of the Prohibition party, and other prominent prohibition workers in the Southern states, and by the Secretary of State in Mississippi, during the months of January and February, 1899: Mississippi has 75 counties; of these 61 are under a state local option, dramshop law; 14 liquor counties only in this commonwealth. Georgia has 137 counties; 113 are under prohibitory law, six or seven of these having dispensaries;—24 liquor counties in Georgia. The Willingham bill, which called for the prohibition of the manufacture and sale of liquor in Georgia, was before the legislature of that state in the winter of 1899. It passed the house by 93 yeas to 65 nays, but was defeated in the senate by a vote of 26 to 14. Kentucky has 119 counties; 73 are under local option, leaving 46 in which there are open saloons; parts of 28 of these counties are " dry." Florida has 44 counties; 20 are under local option; leaving 24 "wet." Alabama has 66 counties; 22 are " dry " and 44 have liquor; however, the legislature, in February, 1899, passed a law which establishes the dispensary in 15 counties, leaving 29 under the control of whiskey. The state of South Carolina is wholly under a rigid dispensary law. Maryland has 23 counties; about half this area is under local option. There are saloons in Tennessee only in incorporated towns; counties without these are dry. Many towns have surrendered their charters in order to annihilate the saloon. There is also a four-mile law which prohibits a dram-shop within that distance of any college, factory, rolling-mill or other chartered institution. It is safe to estimate that much more than half the area of its 36 counties is under prohibitory law. North Carolina has local prohibition in many places in its 96 counties, and is now striving for a rigorous dispensary law. Three-fourths of the state is probably free from the open saloon. Louisiana also has much prohibitory territory spotted about over its 59 parishes, and temperance sentiment is gaining ground steadily. Of the 220 organized counties in Texas 55 have prohibition by local option, and prohibition prevails to such an extent in other counties that " The Texas Liquor Dealer " mourns that one-half the populated area of the state is covered by prohibitory law. These figures show that the white people of the South are very well massed for the temperance cause. It is equally a fact that the ignorant, vicious and purchasable negro vote turns the scale in most of the territory where the open saloon exists. There has been a Prohibition party organization in every Southern state which has done much to create sentiment and annihilate the liquor traffic.

Immediately upon entering the work of the Woman's Christian Temperance Union, I affiliated with the Prohibition party, as it was the only political body in the United States that stood for the protection of the home against the saloon. My brothers and I had stirring arguments on the subject. In their excitement they would walk rapidly up and down the long, old front gallery at the plantation home, and say, " You are the only one of a vast relationship who has gone over to a new political faith. If you and the women associated with you, continue the agitation that has begun you will eventually break up the Democratic party."

One of the stock arguments against woman suffrage is that it is unnecessary for women to vote, as they are represented at the polls by the men of their families. For nearly eleven years I have been the only party Prohibitionist in our household, and in all that time my father and brothers have represented me at the ballot-box by voting a straight Democratic ticket.

Mrs. M. M. Snell and I were appointed by the Prohibition party of Mississippi as delegates to the memorable National Convention which met in Pittsburgh, but, to our regret, found it impossible to attend.

Of course there were physically rough places in my W. C. T. U. pilgrimages through the South,—cold bedrooms and colder halls and churches in winter; frightful heat and suffocating dust in summer; late hours of traveling, excessive fatigue, frequent and prolonged illnesses, often among strangers and uncomfortable surroundings; but, as for real hardships, I have never known them. My trials have been nothing in comparison to those of many women who have given their lives for humanity's uplift in the cause of temperance and prohibition. The leaders of the Woman's Christian Temperance Union—those in the forefront of the battle, are among the bravest of earth. God only can know the crucifixions they have suffered to carry the blessed tidings of this later dispensation to the souls of the sorrowing and the heavy-laden. From the beginning they have been opposed and criticised, and laughed at, but they have gone on their way undaunted, knowing that they were fulfilling a divine commission and were backed by the power and the love of God.

> They did "not hope to be mowers,
>   And to gather the ripe, gold ears,
> Until" they had "first been sowers,
>   And watered the furrows with tears."

None but those who have endured it can know the sting, the bitterness of having to go into homes where there is an utter lack of sympathy; where in each smile there lurks a sneer. None but those who have tried it can realize the hardness of pushing the work in places where people did not care to receive it; of undertaking to banish the wine-glass from the tables of the rich and the beer-mug and the whiskey-flask from the lips of the poor. The constant strife with the liquor traffic and the political power back of it; the standing for principles which the world regards as useless or insulting; the juttings of radicalism—which means Christianity brought down into daily life—against conservatism which often means selfishness. The loneliness of spirit, the bodily fatigue, the unremitting drain on heart and brain and nerve that fill up the days of a worker for the Woman's Christian Temperance Union only the advocates of other great reforms can rightly measure; but they are willing to undergo it all if, by their sufferings, one life can be redeemed or one community brought into touch with God.

The Devonshire coast of England is very dangerous. It is bound by rocks that mean death to any ship that strikes upon them. For many years there have been men employed by the government to walk up and down that sea-girt point to warn passing vessels. They are called life-saving-men. They have worn steep paths into the solid rock, which their faithful, tireless feet have pressed during the time of their ceaseless marchings to and fro. The keen wind bites them and the salt waves drench them and many are swept into the sea; but their places are supplied, the watch is kept up, the signals are given and the ships sail by into their harbors of safety. The leaders of the Woman's Christian Temperance Union are life-saving-women; they walk up and down the rock-bound coast of the world's appetite and ignorance and prejudice waving the danger signal to the souls that pass by on the great deep of temptation. They too have worn steep paths into the stony ground; they too have felt the icy wind and tasted the brine of the salt spray; they too have sunk upon the reefs and have been swept into the sea of eternity. However the watch is kept up; the flag waves on unceasingly; restless, winged feet move unwearied in their ministry; storm-tossed crafts sail by unharmed into the harbor of peaceful lives, under the shadow of the Most High.

CHAPTER XIX

UPON THE HEIGHTS

My rendezvous is appointed, it is certain;
My Lord will be there and wait till I come, on perfect terms;
The great Camerado the lover true for whom I pine, will be
  there.—WALT WHITMAN.

MY three older brothers had left the plantation and
had gone into the wide world to battle with life. The
youngest was at college. On returning from one of my
long campaigns and finding father and mother alone
I said to them, " My first duty is to you. All thought
of leaving home during your life-time will be relin-
quished." The tears sprang quickly to father's eyes,
and he exclaimed, " My daughter, I would pray God
daily to let me die if I thought my living would keep
you from the work of the Woman's Christian Temperance Union." Mother said very quietly but very posi-
tively, " So would I." Of course, under such circumstances it was very easy for me to go.

In 1893 a journey was made to Chicago to take a six
months' course in Bible study and practical Gospel work
in the training school established in that Arabian
Night's city by the great evangelist, Dwight L. Moody.
For months my traveling and speaking had been inces-

sant, and my strength had been so overtaxed, that, soon after arriving, great physical exhaustion followed. Finding it impossible to carry out the proposed program, this institution was left after remaining in it only one month. When vitality began to return lessons in voice culture were taken from a noted specialist. Some time after, on going to a hotel near the World's Fair, in order to visit that wonderful exposition more conveniently, instruction in physical training was received from Baron Possé, a young Swedish nobleman, who was at the head of a successful institution in Boston for the scientific development of the human body. He and his pretty American wife and some of my Southern friends were at the same hotel with me. Among the latter was Miss Clara G. Baer, of New Orleans. She is a native of Louisiana and is another striking illustration of what young Southern women can accomplish. Her childhood was spent in the South, where, as the little " Dixie " of the home, she grew into a girl of much spirit but not robust constitution. Her school life was passed, for the most part, in Kentucky. As she approached womanhood the need of a strong, vigorous physical being was felt more and more. The dream of her life was to be able to do her part in the world's work unencumbered by weakness and days of pain. How to do it became an absorbing question. To leave the anchorage of home and start out alone to find the way was opposed to every family custom, and became the cause of many a controversy with those who loved her. About this time, God sent into her life a woman whose own experience enabled her to grasp this young girl's need. She advised her to go to New

England and take up the work which had so long lain
near her heart, saying: " Remember, we cannot afford
to neglect one opportunity for self-improvement. You
feel the need—leave to God the rest." Acting on this
advice, Miss Baer went to Boston, where she soon
met Baron Nils Possé and his wife. During her
summer work in his classes at Martha's Vineyard they
became warm, personal friends; and when, in the fall,
they invited her to make her home with them, if she decided to remain in Boston, it seemed as though the way
was being pointed out most clearly.

Miss Baer's professional life may be said to have
begun while still a pupil of Baron Possé; for he soon
appointed her to take charge of a large gymnasium for
women at Waltham, Massachusetts. She graduated
from the Possé Gymnasium in the class of '91. Immediately after her graduation she secured the position of
Director of Swedish Gymastics in the Boston School of
Oratory during its summer term. In the fall of that
year, she was made a member of the regular faculty but
was suddenly summoned South by illness in her family.
Being unable to return immediately to Boston, she accepted offers of work at her home in New Orleans, the
positions being Director of the Ladies' Class of the
Southern Athletic Club and of the physical work at
the Quincy school. She was also made a visiting
teacher at Newcomb College and Tulane University.
In the spring of '92 she decided to remain at Newcomb
and was then elected to the faculty. Through her connection with the Woman's Christian Temperance
Union, as State Superintendent of Physical Education,
with the Louisiana Chautauqua and the Peabody Sum-

mer Normals, she has come in touch with the most progressive element, not only in Louisiana, but the entire South. In 1894 she was instrumental in securing the passage of the law which makes physical education a required branch in the public school curriculum, thus placing Louisiana on record as the second state in the Union to take such a step—Ohio being the first. Miss Baer's influence and recognition have passed into the national work of the Woman's Christian Temperance Union and she is now one of the associate superintendents of the department of physical training. She invented the new ball game " Newcomb," and she has also revised " Basket Ball," which she calls " Basquette." Both of these games are copyrighted and published in booklet form. Miss Baer has produced a hand book of gymnastics for the school-room, called " Progressive Lessons in Physical Education," which is in its second edition, the first being published by the School Board of New Orleans for use in connection with her instructions to the teachers of that city. It is now used in their schools. Miss Baer is one of the editors of the " Possé Gymnasium Journal," Boston, Massachusetts, and for the past three years has been lecturer on Medical Gymnastics at the New Orleans Sanitarium and Touro Infirmary Training Schools for Nurses.

During the World's Fair the rare opportunity was granted of meeting many distinguished women from all parts of the earth. The most famous and interesting was Susan B. Anthony, the intrepid advocate of Equal Rights. She was filled, as in her youth, with the inspiration of a mighty purpose. Under its influence she had become the living embodiment of the repressed but unconquerable dignity of the world's womanhood,— calm, self-forgetful, self-sustained. It was a joy to behold her receiving the homage of the public whose criticism and opposition had so persistently followed her in the earlier days but against which she had stood like a wall of granite and had signally overcome. Several years later, when I was passing through Rochester, New York, Miss Anthony invited me to spend a night with her at her home by letter, as follows:

Office of the President, ROCHESTER, N. Y., Aug. 7th 1899.

My Dear Miss Kearney:

I should love to have you over night with us. If you can stay over — telegraph me at once, so that I can announce the fact that we are to have a daughter of Mississippi with us at our next Monday evening "at home". I am sure very many of our suffrage friends will be glad to avail themselves of the opportunity of meeting you, and tell you all about what you are doing, and tell you all about what I want you to do. Which is, as you may guess, to devote yourself wholly to the work of getting the ballot into the hands of the women of Mississippi that they may make of themselves a power to bring about the good they so much desire.

Sincerely & affectionately yours

Susan B. Anthony

On driving up to her dwelling, which was a large brick structure, the great suffragist met me at the carriage and, taking hold of my large traveling-bag, which weighed at least twenty-five pounds, sprang up the front steps and then up the stairway as if she were a young Amazon instead of a woman of seventy-eight years. On my protesting she remarked: " We Northern women are accustomed to waiting on ourselves. It is different with Southerners."

Some distinguished guests had been invited to tea. Miss Anthony was in an animated mood and talked constantly and brilliantly, relating incidents from her earlier experiences in connection with famous men and women who had long since passed away. Before the visitors departed she took a lamp in her hand and bidding us follow, climbed several flights of stairs, finally reaching a sky-chamber.

> This " lady with a lamp shall stand
> In the great history of the land,
> A noble type of good,
> Heroic womanhood! "

From piles of manuscript lying about or packed away securely she drew forth some pages of her biography that had just been completed by her faithful Boswell, Mrs. Ida H. Harper, but which had not yet been delivered to the printing press.

When the hour for retiring came Miss Anthony conducted me to my room and with her own hands prepared the bed, remarking that nothing gave her more pleasure than keeping house. Hanging on the walls of this chamber were time-faded pictures illustrating the horrors of the slave trade. Miss Anthony was an ardent abolitionist and has ceaselessly carried out and on her doctrine of human emancipation.

During my six months' stay in Chicago, in 1893, a most interesting trip was made to Canada, in response to an invitation to deliver an address before the International Convention of the Christian Endeavor Society, which, that year, met in Montreal.

At Kingston we boarded the steamer, *Bohemian,* and had a charming trip down the St. Lawerence, passing the Thousand Islands and successfully shooting the Lachine Rapids.

The day following the adjournment of the convention, I went to Quebec, visiting every point of interest in the quaint old city and for many miles beyond,—from the Plains of Abraham to the beautiful Falls of Montmorency. The greater and more magnificent Falls of Niagara were taken in on my return trip to Chicago.

The year 1893 was memorable for me in many ways. John G. Woolley, the celebrated prohibition and Christian citizenship orator, was met soon after coming back from Canada, and an invitation was received from him to attend a convention, to be held at Rest Island, Minnesota, a short distance from the twin cities, St. Paul and Minneapolis. This lovely spot lies in the heart of the dimpling waters of Lake Pepin which is an expansion of the upper Mississippi. On its wooded banks, in deepest solitude, surrounded by enchanting scenery, Mr. Woolley had established a retreat for men cursed with the appetite for strong drink. They came without money consideration, to seek release, through the grace of Jesus Christ, from the chains that bound them. In the early morning and at twilight those sin-sick men gathered in the bright, east room, where gospel services were conducted by one of the many ministers attending the convention. These were times of tender communing with God, of the birth of souls to the gladness of redemption, of confession of sin and consecration to a higher life.

In that restful, blessed place my soul began to hunger more for God. I yearned for a closer touch, a deeper knowledge, a truer hand-clasp, a safer walk with my Redeemer than had yet been realized. Daily the burden was with me of the consciousness that my religious life needed a clearer coloring, a finer texture, a more abiding strength. A desire to see God " face to face, " to talk with Him upon the heights was ever present. Hours were spent in agonizing prayer and passionate weeping. At length the glory of God shone upon me and there came a full baptism of the Holy Ghost. Joy and peace had followed my conversion, but as the years had gone by with their increasing responsibilities the sweetness of entire dependence upon God had departed and the old deadness had begun to creep over my soul. With this renewal of tryst with my Lord, there came again the same rest and gladness that accompanied my first meeting with Christ; but it was deeper and calmer, and mingled with a mysterious, wonderful outpouring of the Spirit. Some writer has said: " It is well to take time to mend one's friendships." It has been proven in my experience that it is necessary, at intervals along life's journey, to make fresh consecrations, to renew our covenants with God.

CHAPTER XX

How can we tell what coming people are aboard the ships that be sailing to us now from the unknown seas?
—CHAS. DICKENS.

ON returning from Chicago, in November, 1893, my work of organization and lecturing was resumed in the Southern states and carried on without interruption until May, 1895. At that time the State Convention of the Mississippi Woman's Christian Temperance Union met in Natchez. Mrs. L. S. Mount, who had served so long and faithfully in the presidency, resigned, and the honor of filling her place was conferred upon me. Within three weeks after, I received a cablegram from Miss Willard, who was then in England, asking me to come at once to London. An International Convention of the Woman's Christian Temperance Union was to be held there at which she desired me to be present. Father and mother insisted that the call be accepted. A formal resignation of my office as State President was made, as the length of my sojourn abroad would be uncertain. The fact of having a vice-president-at-large insured that the machinery of the state organization would move without break. The health of my oldest brother had failed two years before and he had returned to the old home; he had become so much better that all of us thought he was on the road to complete recovery. Knowing he could never be sufficiently robust for active business, it was planned for him to live with father and mother.

In a short time every preparation for my departure was finished. After a tender farewell and " God speed " from my dear ones, I was soon traveling to New York, with a heart full of thanksgiving to my Heavenly Father for His marvellous blessings. The dream of my life was about to be realized,—a trip to Europe was close at hand.

Several days were spent at Prohibition Park, Staten Island, attending the farewell meetings which were held in honor of the delegates from the United States and Canada to the World's W. C. T. U. Convention in London. At last we stood beside the ship that was to carry us across the ocean. The time for it to move off had almost arrived; but my trunk had not come. My uneasiness grew with the flying moments; still it did not appear. A dear friend who stood by me, noticing my anxiety, said softly, again and again, " You must learn to trust God in the dark! " At the last moment, the longed-for baggage arrived.

On June 5th, at 4 P. M., the steamer *Berlin* moved out from New York harbor in a glow of sunshine. Hundreds of friends stood on the pier waving their handkerchiefs to the passengers, who leaned over the bulwarks and watched them with yearning eyes until the growing distance hid them from view. Then followed a rush for chairs, a diving into trunks for suitable clothing for the voyage, greeting of state-room companions, and general adjustment to environments. Later the dining-saloon was the source of attraction, to some of us for the first and last time. "Life on the ocean wave" was delightful for fifteen hours to me. During the night a heavy fog settled upon the waters, the fog-horn blew shrilly every few moments, and the ship moved slowly. The fog and the horn-blowing continued through two following days. The captain stayed at his post during all the weary hours without a moment's sleep, having his meals carried up to him. He feared coming in contact with "ships that pass in the night." During all this time the ocean was calm and unruffled, but black and sullen looking. The third morning brought the sunshine, which continued. Sea-sickness came with the dawn of the first day. The passengers sat on deck, wrapped in heavy rugs, too miserable to speak, too inert to move. Deck stewards moved to and fro dispensing beef tea and hard-tack, arranging head-rests, and making the situation easy for the sufferers.

The monotony was broken Sunday morning by services held at 11 o'clock, when a sermon was preached, and at night another meeting was conducted. The ship, which had been making good time, began to move slowly when the deep sea was reached beyond Newfoundland, as icebergs float beneath the water in this latitude, and to strike one means fatality.

There was a glorious company on board—lecturers, ministers, writers, singers, and (inglorious) a French variety troupe. Every day the W. C. T. U. women observed the noon-tide hour with prayer. In the evenings entertainments were held in the dining-saloon when there would be music, lectures and recitations.

In the early morning, the last day at sea, a flock of sea-gulls denoted that we were nearing the shores of England; soon we were sailing by the Scilly Islands. News of the arrival of the *Berlin* was received immediately at the first light-house, telegraphed to Southampton and cabled thence to New York. Land's End was later reached, bringing to remembrance Charles Wesley and the lines he wrote while standing there:

> " Lo! on a narrow neck of land,
> 'Twixt two unbounded seas I stand."

Then we sailed along the Cornish coast and after awhile caught glimpses of hawthorn hedges, growing grain and stately dwellings. There were a number of little boats with crimson sails floating on the water and numerous brigs and steamers. Sky and sea and earth were in fullest harmony. Beautiful! beautiful! beautiful!

Friday night, June 14th, we anchored in port at Southampton. Early next morning some one knocked at my state-room door. Opening it I was joyously greeted by Miss Jessie Ackerman, who had come down from London to meet the delegates to the World's W. C. T. U. Convention, for which organization she had just completed her second circuit of the globe as " Round-the-World Missionary." She accompanied me to the home of her hostess and mine, the well-known Quakeress preacher and author, Hannah Whitall Smith, whose " Christian's Secret of a Happy Life " has had more editions and been printed in more languages than almost any other American book.   Soon we were in the cars, gliding swiftly through bright fields of wheat and crimson poppies, past charming little villages, clean and picturesque, to the great metropolis.

The home of Hannah Whitall Smith is one of the headquarters of intellectual freedom in London. Everything in her household is beautifully attuned to the law of grace and beauty; even the meals are announced by an exquisite strain of music proceeding from some mysterious source.   Among the other guests in this hospitable home were Mrs. Margaret Bottome, President of the International Order of King's Daughters; Frau Kamer and Frau Gezyski, elegant ladies from Germany, Miss Alli Trigg, of Finland, and Madame Selmer of Denmark.   There had never been such immense and enthusiastic meetings held in the interest of the temperance reform in Great Britain as those that took place in London during the week that followed our arrival.

Sunday morning, June 16th, 1895, I received the following little note from Miss Willard, which was sent by a special messenger.   It was headed 94 Ashley Gardens.

" DEAR BELLE,

" Howdy ! So glad ! You have been elected the only new (spick and span) round-the-world missionary. You are to speak fifteen minutes this P. M.   Meet us. Come with H. W. S. to the platform.   Ever thine,

" SISTER FRANCES."

That afternoon I had the great honor and privilege of speaking in City Temple, better known as the church of Dr. Joseph Parker, with Miss Willard, Lady Henry Somerset and " Mother Stewart " of Crusade fame. Nearly two-hundred meetings were addressed by the White Ribbon speakers in London that day. Afterward it was my happy lot to speak on five occasions during this visit in England's Capital, the most notable being at the superb international demonstration in Albert hall, which is said to be the largest auditorium in the world. An audience of ten-thousand assembled and it was stated that tickets of admission had to be refused to tens of thousands more. The National Convention of the British Woman's Temperance Association was in session June 17-18. It was composed of over six-hundred earnest, intelligent women from England, Scotland and Wales.

On Wednesday, June 19th, 1895, Miss Willard opened the World's Convention of the Woman's Christian Temperance Union in Queen's Hall with 234 delegates, representing twenty-four nations, and with members of fraternal delegates from kindred societies. A morning conference the following day closed the business proceedings of the third Biennial Convention of the best organized and largest body of women on earth.

The Lord Mayor of London gave a reception to the international delegates, during the World's Convention and, on June 21st, Lady Henry Somerset received at her famous country residence, the Priory at Reigate, Surrey. Hundreds of women from nearly every clime were rapidly transported from the heat and dust of London to the historic edifice which " her ladyship " had just refitted most elegantly for the coming of age of her only son. After the guests were cordially greeted by Lady Henry and Miss Willard, they spent the remainder of the day in wandering over the beautiful grounds and in enjoying a study of the antique furnishings of the Priory in which were found rare paintings and tapestry, coats-of-mail and other curious relics of a long line of noble ancestry.

Every day since receiving the appointment of round-the-world missionary I had been in an agony of unrest, and waited constantly on God in prayer for guidance. It required a hard and desperate struggle before my duty was made clear. My desire was strong to *go*, but the divine leadings *not* to go were at last very definite and infinitely stronger. My physical strength had been terribly depleted by six years of continuous public work and travel, and the realization was forced upon me that not enough vitality was left to undertake the arduous labors of a missionary in foreign lands. Besides, there was an abiding consciousness that it was not the will of my Heavenly Father that I should go at that time. The invisible but real hands of God were felt pushing me away from the acceptance of this commission. On the ship, going over, this message was sent me by the Father, but its import was not understood for many months after: " Beloved, think it not strange concerning the fiery trial which is to try you as though some strange thing happened unto you: but rejoice inasmuch as ye are partaker(s) of Christ's sufferings; that, when His glory shall be revealed, ye may be glad also with exceeding joy."

On the day the reception was given at the Priory I asked to be allowed to appear before the Executive Committee of the World's W. C. T. U., which met in the afternoon in an upper chamber. After explaining the reason for my action a formal resignation was made of the office to which I had been elected. Subsequent events proved the wisdom of my determination.

CHAPTER XXI

ON THE CONTINENT

Like as a plank of driftwood
Tossed on the watery main
Another plank, encounters, meets, touches, parts again;
So, tossed and drifting ever
On life's unresting sea
Men meet and greet and sever
Parting eternally.—SANSCRIT, B. C., 1600.

IMMEDIATELY after the adjournment of the World's
great convention Miss Willard and Lady Henry Somerset commissioned me to represent the Woman's Christian Temperance Union at the International Congress of
Christian Workers at Grindelwald, Switzerland, and my
departure was made at once for that place with a party
of friends from the United States. Crossing the Channel, which was smooth and beautiful, we landed at
Calais and were soon passing through the sunny slopes
of *la belle France*. About dusk we reached the town
where Joan of Arc met her unhappy fate. A wretched
night was spent with seven ladies locked up in a compartment in a continental car, which is such a horror to
all travelers who have ever enjoyed the luxury of a
sleeper on our great American lines of railway. Next
morning we passed over into Swiss territory. We be-

came aware at once that we had gotten into finer atmosphere and on higher ground. At noon we crossed Lake Thun, which lies like a gem in the heart of the great mountains that surround it.

Grindelwald is a famous resort high up in the Burnese Alps. The Jungfrau and the Matterhorn keep eternal watch over the hamlet and its kindly, simple people. It was here that Dr. Henry Lunn, the editor of " The Review of the Churches," had established a European Chautauqua, the leading purpose of which was to promote church unity. The town consists of several hotels, a few stores, many bazaars where curios are sold to tourists, and a few charming " chalets." Among the last is that of Madame D'Aubigne, the wife of the great writer. The adjacent hills are covered with the quaint huts of the peasants. A little Protestant church, antique in structure, occupies a prominent place, and adds to the generally striking effect. In it our meetings were held to advance the temperance cause, and here I had the pleasure of speaking.

For four delightful, never-to-be-forgotten days we stayed in those rarified regions, growing nearer to God with every breath. At sunrise, parties began excursions through the mountains, some riding on horseback, others in carriages or on railways. We went to the very edge of glaciers, and looked down into the clefts of seemingly interminable blue ice; climbed to the tops of peaks; walked over beds of snow and watched avalanches fall in a splendor of misty whiteness. The women work in the fields as regularly as the men. Often they were seen hitched to carts pulling heavy loads of hay, or bearing burdens on their backs. Once I saw a man between two women drawing a wagon.

While at Grindelwald a cordial invitation was sent by Lady Henry Somerset, through Miss Willard, to occupy a room for as long as I desired for rest and re-cuperation at the former's *Chalet Villors,* near Aigle, not far from Lausanne, but I decided to take a tour with friends through several countries of Europe in-stead of resting.

From Grindelwald we went to Interlaken and there took a boat and passed up Lake Brienz. Soon we began to ascend the Alps, going over the Brunig Pass. Just before we reached Hergiswyl, we gained a view of Mt. Rigi. Beyond, nestling close to the ideally beautiful lake that bears its name, is the city of Lucerne. In this heavenly place we tarried all too short a while, then journeyed to Geneva, by whose borders Lake Leman stretches its shimmering length; the Rhone, blue and placid, winds through its heart; the Alpine range reaches to the very edge of its quaint old streets. Mont Blanc rears its majestic head in full view—pink in the flush of the early dawn, pure white at noontide, or red with evening cloud-glories. I have noticed that the highest mountains always catch first the rays of sun-light in the mornings and are the last to retain them in rosy tints upon their snow-crowned heights when the shades of night draw near. So it is with those lives that are in nearest touch with God. They are the first to receive the inspiration of His great thoughts and the last to reflect them, standing above the multitude in their lonely grandeur and translating to the world beneath the holy will of the Father concerning them.

Geneva is a great educational center. The academy organized by Calvin, and which was afterward honored by having John Knox among its first students, has grown into a university and has become the Mecca of progresssive Protestants on account of its broad spirit. Women are admitted to its lectures on perfect equality with men. Consequently the former are becoming more numerous every year. After making a trip to the Castle of Chillon, visiting the home of Voltaire in the little French town of Ferney, and seeing the elegant chateau at Coppet where Madame de Stael was banished by Napoleon for being too much interested in politics, and different historic points in Geneva—among them the house where Jean Jacques Rousseau was born—we passed into Italy.

Turin was the first place at which we stopped, then Pisa. Despite the subjection that is taught women by the Catholic church in Europe it is pleasant to note signs of the breaking up of old forms of social crystallization. In Pisa there is a normal school conducted on a co-educational basis; and I was told that a number of women were there studying medicine. This was more interesting to me than the leaning tower and the swinging lamp from which Galileo gained his inspiration.

Before Genoa was reached, we approached the Apennines and for a long distance sped through their magnificent heights and smiling valleys. At the city whose name is evermore linked with that of Columbus, begins the wonderful road along the Riviera. We gained here our first sight of the Mediterranean, and for many miles skirted close to its rock-bound coast.

En route to Rome, in our compartment, were two ladies of our company besides myself, an old Italian woman and two foreign men. We had to make ourselves as comfortable as circumstances allowed, which meant that some slept sitting upright, some with head on seat and feet on valise, while others watched and slumbered not. At twelve the two men drew out their bottles and drank heavily, then lighted their cigars and smoked. This interesting performance was repeated at short intervals until the day dawned. There was a streak of sunlight through the reeking air, short staccato snorts from my companions in distress, a rubbing of eyes, a stretching of muscles, an exchange of miserable glances, an outlook through the open window to the shining waters of the Mediterranean, soon a dash across the yellow Tiber, and we were in the Eternal city. Rome, like heaven, is a place to be striven for, to dream over and hunger for; but it is better to leave to the imagination than to attempt to put into words the measure of its treasures, old and new, its historic suggestion and the power of the awful and majestic march of the ages which echoes from its sacred hills.

From Rome we went to Naples, then to Pompeii. Climbing to the top of the highest point of observation upon the walls of the once lava-buried city, we obtained a fine view of the surrounding landscape. Before us lay the Bay of Naples, placid in the July sun; beyond it the

Apennines; on the further shore the towns of Castella-
mare, Herculaneum, and beautiful Sorrento, the birth-
place of Tasso; to the right Naples; in the rear, Vesu-
vius, sending out its volume of never-ending smoke.

Venice answered in full all the dreams that I ever had
of its beauties. On leaving there we traveled to Flor-
ence, where, unfortunately, only a short time could be
spent in the art galleries, studying the great works of
the old masters who have rendered the city famous, and
in threading the thoroughfares made historic by illus-
trious men and women.

In Milan, the white marble Cathedral was, of course,
the centre of our desires, after that the refectory of the
Dominican Convent, near the church of Sta. Maria della
Grazia, where is found all that remains of " The Last
Supper," Leonardi da Vinci's masterpiece, a fresco,
which is almost obliterated.

The innate tact and grace of Italian people is delightful. One day our party of W. C. T. U. women were
crowded in a railway compartment. The only men
present were our conductor, a cultured young English-
man, the son of the Bishop of Winchester, and an
elegant looking young Italian gentleman of the higher
class. The latter could not speak a word of English,
and was an entire stranger to the rest of us. As we
entered he was smoking, ignoring the fact that the carriage was not intended for that purpose. The ladies
gave evidence of disapprobation; but the unconscious
sinner smoked on ignorant of the misery he was creat-
ing. Finally our escort leaned toward him and said in
the native tongue: " Will you please discard your

cigarette? The ladies object to it." The Italian looked around perfectly amazed. I presume it was the first time in his whole life that he had been made aware of the fact that women objected to smoking, as so many indulge in the habit in Europe. When the Italian saw the expression on the faces of his fellow-passengers he colored to the roots of his black, curly hair, and immediately threw away the offending cigarette; anxious to atone for the discomfort he had unwittingly caused, he sprang to his feet, and, opening a large wicker basket in the rack above him, took therefrom a beautiful lemon with a long branch and leaves attached, and, with a graceful bow, handed it to the lady opposite.

After a day and night's continuous travel from Milan, we arrived in Paris. Gay, charming Paris! the loveliest and wickedest city on earth. There is an irresistible fascination in the *sans souci* of these impulsive, happy-hearted human beings. There is joy and lightness in the very air, that takes hold of one unconsciously; but when we think of the immorality and atheism under it all, we are conscious of a pain and a pathos unspeakable. If there is a place in the world against which all the artillery of Christianity should be leveled, that place is Paris. Now there are only feeble rush-lights in the midnight darkness. One-hundred and fifty Mc-Call Missions are scattered over France; there are thirty in Paris. One night, after walking down the brilliantly lighted boulevards with a party of friends, we strolled into one of these quiet little rooms. On the wall opposite us was written, in French, " I am the Resurrection and the Life." The minister who con-

ducted the evening service read passages from the Bible
and announced the hymns, none of which we understood. When we had almost decided in despair to retire,
the organ pealed forth the familiar strain, " Whosoever
Will May Come," and we lifted our American voices in
praise, with their sweet French tones. Finally, we
joined in singing together that dear old consecration
hymn, " I am Thine, O, Lord," and left with thanksgiving to God that there was a place, however small, in
the great city, into which those who love Him and
serve Him can go apart for awhile and rest.

Miss de Broen, a young woman from Holland of
wealth and leisure, while traveling for pleasure on the
continent in 1871, arrived in Paris during the terrible
days of the last Commune. She was so impressed by
the horrors which she witnessed that she decided to remain and help to alleviate the sufferings of the people in
the Belleville district, the scene of the bloody butchery.
There was begun at once that beautiful mission work
that has made her name blessed in the hearts of thousands of human beings. For nearly twenty-five years
she has stood an unwavering light in the darkness of
atheistic gloom, carrying forward her vast undertaking
with a trust that has never once abated. Terrible sickness followed in the wake of the siege. Miss de Broen
established a medical hospital, where the sufferers could
be administered to free of cost. After the Revolution
ended it was continued for the poor in Belleville; but
through all the years it had been resorted to by many
from the heart of Paris, the average annual attendance
being as great as 30,000. In supplying the bodily wants

of these needy people, no opportunity had been neglected of bringing their sin-sick souls to the personal knowledge of the Divine Physician, who came to " bear our infirmities."   Out of this enterprise there had grown a training school for girls, sewing classes, day and night schools, mothers' meetings, a gospel mission hall, where regular Sunday services were held, beside Bible classes, prayer meetings and temperance meetings.   A large proportion of Miss de Broen's time was spent in visiting the poor and sick, and distributing tracts and Bibles. I shall never forget the pathos in the voices of the men and the women, who stretched out their hands in an imploring way to her, saying, " If you please, madame," for the gospel leaflets she carried as we walked through the streets of Belleville.   One day I dined with Miss de Broen and afterward spoke at her mission.   She urged me to stay and lecture to the English-speaking people of Paris, offering me a home and a salary, but it was impossible to accept for the same reasons that prevented me from going around the world as a W. C. T. U. missionary.   It was a wonderful opening fraught with gracious possibilities for the spread of the blessed doctrine of total abstinence and the gospel of our Lord. I pray God that some strong young woman who reads these words may feel impelled to go; if not to Paris, to some other field of mission work for the Master.

On my return from Paris several days were spent in London.   After going out to Windsor Castle, Hampton Court and many other points of interest, I bade good-bye to the friends who had been with me on the continent and began a journey alone through

Ireland. Happy hours were spent in its leading cities, in riding over its picturesque mountains and in skimming over the surface of the beautiful lakes of Killarney.

Leaving Ireland I went directly to Scotland. Edinburgh, the historic, the romantic, was the goal of my heart's desire. At sunset that glorious old city was reached, with its ancient castle, Holyrood Palace, and Princes street, incomparable for beauty—bathed in light—its crags and rocks, its hills and stretch of sea.

Of all the fascinating spots around Edinburgh, the most charming is the home of Sir Walter Scott. A short ride on the cars brings us to Melrose, where we take an omnibus for a four-mile jaunt through the country of Abbottsford, the baronial castle that was the pride of the heart of " the grand old man " of Scotland.

Melrose Abbey was next explored and a trip made through the Trosachs, the region of the " Lady of the Lake," the most captivating section of all Scotland. Long coach drives were taken through the wildest, grandest parts of the Highlands, and two boat rides; one across Loch Katrine, the other down Loch Lomond.

CHAPTER XXII

THE SORROW.

Behold, the Lord our God hath shewed us His glory and His greatness, and we have heard His voice out of the midst of the fire; we have seen this day that God doth talk with man and he liveth.—DEUT. 5 : 24.

THE last week in August I sailed from Scotland for the United States, and after an uneventful voyage arrived in New York, spending some time there and on Staten 'Island, at the latter place addressing a public meeting.

It was too early in the season to return with safety to the South, but a strong presentiment of coming sorrow so impressed itself upon me that it was impossible to shake it off, or to attempt to do any work, or to entertain any thought but that of going home. For the first time in my life a foreboding was yielded to and the last week of September found me on the plantation at Vernon. I was shocked to find my brother, whom I had left with every assurance of returning health, frightfully altered—stamped with the seal of death. Neither he, nor any one, seemed to realize the hopelessness of his condition, but a physician was in constant attendance.

Although scarcely able to stand, he wandered about

the house restlessly, silent, his attenuated figure the
shadow of his former fine physique, his face sad and un-
smiling with a touch of the awfulness of eternity upon
it. The next Sabbath he was unable to arise. As I
waited by his bedside he looked at me calmly, his blue
eyes full of the old love of his boyhood days, and
actuated by the same unselfish spirit that had characterized his life, he said apologetically, " I am a little too
weak to get up this morning, sister." Several days of
great suffering followed. At last the knowledge that
death was close at hand came to him. He asked mother
to pray. " If life is given me I will show the world
what it means to be a Christian man," he said. Oh!
the heart-break of that hour! In the holy watches of
those days and nights surely he had an understanding
with God, Who had said so lovingly through His Son,
" Come unto me all ye that are weary and heavy laden
and I will give you rest."

In one week's time, my brother died. There are
moments when one cannot weep, nor speak, nor pray,—
only be quiet before God. This was my first great sorrow. My faculties were dazed in the presence of death's
awful mystery. How strange every one seemed! How
weird the trees, the flowers, the sunlight! I was alone
with our dead. He would soon be taken away from the
old home to come back no more forever. *Forever?* O,
God! why should we be put in this sorrowing, unsatisfying world to struggle and to suffer—to grope, and
never to *know?* All the fought-for peace of years fled
from me; all the trustfulness, the acceptance slipped
away in the darkness and horror of those hours.

Twice in my life there has been felt the personal presence of God. Into that chamber of silence, shrouded in the desolation that only death can bring, He came to me; softly, swiftly, clearly the footsteps of my Lord were heard; suddenly the room was filled with His glory. Distinctly as if a human voice had spoken there fell upon my awakened sense the blessed words, " Peace, be still!" A holy calm descended upon me, a strange, sweet gladness. I went out rejoicing and praising God.

After awhile our beloved was taken away. The mourning little company filed its way across the autumn fields, aglow with October sunshine, to our old family burial-ground, near by, in the heart of the deep, still woods. The long shadows flickered across the open grave, and the fading light fell in golden glints about it. My tears had all been shed, a divine, inexplicable joy possessed my being. I wanted to sing, to speak! My soul was on wings, and thrilled with the triumphant refrain, " I know that my Redeemer liveth," while the divine undertone of Christ's assurance echoed back, " I am the resurrection, and the life: Whosoever believeth in Me, though he were dead, yet shall he live." " Whosoever!" *He believed.* Thank God!

Two days after my brother's burial I was lying in the shadow of death with typhoid fever. The doctor looked at me with sad eyes full of apprehension. " You are very ill," he said, " but you will not die." " O, that is quite certain," was my instant reply. " My life work is not yet finished; the call will not come for me to go until my destiny is completed."

The fiery furnace of sickness and sorrow left me

stronger in mind and more in love with God than in all my life before. In the days of convalescence my studies were resumed with eager vehemence. As soon as physical strength returned, my public work was renewed and continued from March until November. I was radiantly happy, and my efforts were crowned with unusual success. Numbers of new friends came into my life, splendid audiences greeted me and many adherents were gained for the cause of righteousness to which my time and enthusiasm were devoted.

At the close of the spring campaign in Mississippi a tour was made through Georgia where the privilege was granted of standing on ground rendered sacred by John Wesley in the days of his early ministry in America. In going to Charlotte, North Carolina, a visit was paid to the gentle, sweet-faced widow of Stonewall Jackson. She had been a member of the white-ribbon army for years, and spoke with pride of her distinguished husband's total abstinence principles, quoting his famous remark, " I fear a glass of liquor more than the bullets of the enemy."

Soon after leaving North Carolina, the historic capital of the Southern Confederacy was seen for the first time. My hostess carried me to every place of interest in the charming old city,—the house that Jefferson Davis occupied while president of the seceded states, now used as a Confederate museum; the residence of Robt. E. Lee, owned at present by the Virginia Historical Society; St. Paul's Episcopal church, where these two famous leaders worshipped and whose pews, at the time, were draped with Confederate colors and dec-

orated with laurel wreaths; St. John's chapel, built in
1771, where Patrick Henry made his immortal demand;
the stone house in which Washington and Lafayette
held their conference; the elegant monuments erected in
honor of the soldiers and sailors, General Lee and other
heroes, and Holywood cemetery, where Monroe, Tyler,
J. E. B. Stuart and Jefferson Davis lie buried. At this
beautiful place of interment a striking memorial has
been erected by the Ladies' Association in memory of
the Confederate dead. It consists of a vast pile of
stones laid in the form of an obelisk. At its completion
it was found to be very difficult to put the cap-stone
in place,—many trying and all failing. Finally it was
announced by the state that freedom would be granted
to any convict in the penitentiary who could adjust it.
The opportunity was too precious to be lost and one of
these unfortunates gained the double triumph.

The Ex-Confederates were having a great reunion
during my visit to Richmond. The city was filled with
men dressed in gray uniforms, tattered and time-stained.
Among these were some old negroes who had served
throughout the civil war with their masters. Nothing
more pathetic could be imagined than the happiness
they evinced moving among the veterans and wearing
the badges of the regiments in which they served as
proudly as on the day in the 60's when they marched
away to the battle fields.

Day and night the crowds filled the vast auditorium
of the Exposition building which was decorated with
war pictures and battle flags. There were glowing

speeches by prominent Southern orators, interspersed with martial music. The old songs were sung that had brightened many a camp-fire; the " rebel yell " was given,—at first short and sharp, but finally swelling into a deafening roar, the enthusiasm increasing with every demonstration.

There was no exhibition of bitterness on any occasion. The address of the Northern Soldier received an ovation. There was deathless loyalty in every Southerners' heart to the spirit under which the war had been fought but with it was an unquestioning allegiance to the Union. The stars and stripes were dearer to them, even in that hour of tender reminiscence, than their own conquered banners. I wept with the old warriors in memory of their " Lost Cause; " but there was profound thankfulness in my heart that the Civil War ended as it did; that fraternity was restored; that no longer was there a North and a South but an undivided country; a united purpose, under one flag, to work out our sublime destiny—the development for the world of the principles of self-government.

Since then, the war between the United States and Spain has been fought. The North and the South have stood shoulder to shoulder in the movement at El Caney, in the furious charge up the hill of San Juan, in the sinking of the Spanish fleet at Santiago and in the immortal victory at Manila. Heroes of both sections perished together on the Maine, and lie buried side by side in the trenches of Cuba and the Philippines.   The forces of fraternity have culminated in the Spanish-American war; but in all the years since Lee surrendered his sword to Grant at Appomattox numerous agencies have been at work to effect the solidity of the American people and to unify the great Republic.

CHAPTER XXIII

THE FAR WEST AND ALASKA

And who commanded (and the silence came),
Here let the billows stiffen and have rest !
God ! let the torrents, like a shout of nations,
Answer, and let the ice-plains echo, God !
— COLERIDGE.

AFTER visiting the University of Virginia and the
famous home of Thomas Jefferson, " Monticello," at
Charlottesville, Virginia, the remainder of the summer
was spent at Mountain Lake Park, Maryland, Old
Orchard Beach, Maine, where W. C. T. U. work was
done, and on the coast of Narragansett Bay, near New-
port. Lecture engagements were filled in the fall of
1896 in the state of New York, where pleasant visits
were made to the United States Military Academy, at
West Point, Vassar College, at Poughkeepsie, and many
delightful trips up and down the Hudson were enjoyed.
Addresses were made in New Jersey and in all the New
England states except Vermont. Everywhere I was
received with unlimited cordiality, and was the subject
of as much generous hospitality and loving kindness as
was ever lavished upon me in the South.

The following spring a lecturing and organizing tour
was begun in March, that continued until the middle
of December, through the far West. Never until this

journey had I realized the immensity of the distances in this great country of ours. With the dawn of the morning following my leave taking from Forth Worth, Texas, I found myself skirting the great American desert traveling up the Pecos Valley in New Mexico. The country to El Paso is an unchangeable, sandy valley with mountain ranges on either side, bare and dusty looking. Not a human habitation is in sight, except wigwams huddled on the glowing desert at frightful distances from each settlement. These were occupied by Indians. Here, as elsewhere in this region, nothing is seen growing except the mesquite bushes, Spanish daggers, and numerous varieties of cactus.

As soon as I got to El Paso I entered a street car to pay a visit to the old Mexican town, Juarez, which is just across the Rio Grande, with the purpose of seeing the ancient church Guadaloupe, which dates from 1549. It was my plan to make a missionary temperance tour through Mexico on my return in December, but afterward I concluded to defer the journey until more time was at my command.

On leaving El Paso the train swept through the heart of the desert with its blinding glories, mammoth cacti with crimson blossoms, a few lonely birds beating their wings in the air, and the inevitable line of mountains about us. It seemed like a foretaste of heaven to glide in from the arid plains of Arizona to the cool, green regions of California, with its fields of barley and wheat, orchards of various fruits, and mountains softened with grass and shrubs—all bathed in evening light with the peculiar glow in it that rests on the hills and valleys of Italy.

Soon after my arrival in San Francisco, accompanied by an ensign from the Salvation Army and a Christian lady friend, I went down one night into the depths of Chinatown. This is a section of San Francisco that is inhabited wholly by the Chinese, who, true to their instincts, have packed themselves into every available niche. Within ten blocks 20,000 of these Mongolians are found—human beings of every variety wedged in with poultry and animals, flesh and vegetables. We went into the opium dives, entering dark, forbidding, rambling old houses, and after meandering around in shadowy courts and murky passages arrived at tiny rooms full of rags and filth and fumes, and saw stretched out on loathsome cots specimens of humanity that had once been called men, but at present looked more like spirits from Hades; bodies thin and scrawny, the yellow skin like parchment drawn over the grinning bones; small, sleepy almond eyes glistening under shaggy brows that beetled from bare, knotty foreheads; a mass of blue-black hair coiled at the back of the head; all—bones, skin, eyes and hair piled up in the middle of the bed—smoking. A flickering candle was standing on a little table close by the couch. Beside the light was a small jar containing a dark, gummy substance, which we soon discovered to be opium. As we entered one of these dens the smoker grunted a recognition and closed his eyes. In his hand he held a long-stemmed pipe, with the mouth-piece glued between his lips. Suddenly he sat up, and, leaning towards the table, he took a small wiry instrument, and, digging up a speck of opium from the jar, he punched it into his pipe, the opening of which was at the end of the bowl, and holding it over the flames sucked the stem vigorously until the opium puffed and fizzed. Two or three whiffs, and all was over. At once the smoker repeated the operation, then again and again, looking at us appealingly at the end of each performance for a piece of money. We endured the sight of the degradation as long as we could, then walked away filled with disgust.

After leaving the opium dens we went to the Chinese theatre. It was filled to overflowing. On the main floor were men, all sitting on the back of the seats, and each fellow smoking like a steam engine. The air was so full of the fumes as to almost suffocate one and so cloudy as to obscure the vision. Penned off in the boxes were the women. As soon as we entered we were met by an usher and marched up, not to a reserved seat, but on the stage, in the midst of the actors. In astonishment there we sat, and gazed with awe upon the horrible creatures dressed to resemble nothing on earth nor "in the waters under the earth." Painted faces and naked chests decorated with skins and tinsel, marching to and fro beating pans and drums, and screeching, whooping and dancing. In the midst of the pandemonium we sat and gazed, and the smoking Chinamen in the audience sat and gazed at us. It was a midsummer night's horror.

In walking through the uncertain streets in the flicker of the faintly glimmering lights we saw poor little Chinese women dressed in gaudy clothes, with rouged cheeks, hurrying by, and others of their unfortunate sisters looking from curtained windows down upon the surging crowd of men upon the streets below. Poor little sparrows! God pity them!

From the theatre we went to the joss house—the Chinese place of worship. It is a large building with an up-stairs balcony. The furnishings are rich. Idols, looking like monsters, are standing about, and there are heavy curtains, and inscriptions in gold, altars towering nearly to the ceiling, and great basins where the ashes are caught that fall from burning the sacred sticks. There was the " holy of holies " that the foot of a Christian is not allowed to enter.

We visited the handsome stores and watched with amusement the lordly air and stately tread of the wealthy merchants as they walked up and down their establishments bartering away their costly wares. While standing in one of these stores a little Chinese boy six years old came in and asked his father a question; then followed an animated conversation. The merchant, turning to us, said: " My little son. He likee Mellican shoes. I give him a pair, but he will not carry paper bundles on the street. He do not think it high-toned. " It is hard to Americanize the Chinaman. In spite of missions and direct contact with our civilization, he retains his oriental dress and heathenish customs.

My first view of the Pacific was gained at Inspiration Point, a lofty eminence to the west of San Francisco overlooking the Golden Gate, the beautiful bay and the mountains. The trip from San Francisco to Portland takes one through the delightful Shasta region. The scenery is magnificent every step of the way as far north as Ashland—an almost unbroken stretch of mountainous country that grows in grandeur until the border line of California and Oregon is passed. Mt. Shasta stands out like a mighty giant for hundreds of miles, robed in snow; cold, changeless, full of majesty and mystery. From Portland I sailed down the Columbia river nearly to its mouth, gaining glimpses of Mt. Hood and Mt. Rainier along the route.

Passing from Oregon, I went into Washington, visiting first the interesting little city of Vancouver, and after a short, delightful stay at the capital, made a boat trip on Puget Sound to Tacoma.

During the first week of July, 1897, I took passage on the elegant steamship, *Queen,* departing for Alaska. Going from Seattle to Sitka is like sailing up a wide, smooth river, with all the joys of a sea voyage without any of its discomforts. On either side is an unbroken stretch of magnificent scenery that transcends all description. Every view is full of exquisite beauty, or replete with grandeur. The trip to Alaska is the summer tour par excellence, sought by tourists from all parts of the world, and pronounced by them to be incomparable.

To convey an adequate conception of the mammoth size of Alaska, it is said that if one were to stand twenty miles to the westward of San Francisco, he would be just half-way in the possessions of the Federal government. Alaska is larger than all the states that would be included in a line drawn east from Chicago to the Atlantic, and south as far as the Gulf of Mexico.

The rivers of Alaska are among the longest, and it has the highest mountains, the largest glaciers, the most numerous bays, straits, sounds and channels, and the richest gold and silver mines on two continents. The wonderful revelations among all the other wonders of this wonder-land are the glaciers. On the trip to Sitka the first of these of any importance that is passed is the Patterson. After that comes the Davidson, then the Windome, and at last the Muir, that marvelous inland sea more than one hundred fathoms deep, which is renowned as one of the most astonishing developments in the natural world. There are said to be ten other glaciers in Alaska as large as the Muir, one twice as large, besides many small ones. Now for the Muir itself. Imagine, facing a body of placid water, great colonnades of ice forming a crescent two miles in length, 250 feet high at the centre, and sloping gently down at either end to 150 feet. Imagine this frozen mass fashioned in the most fairy-like forms and dream-creations—chiseled grottoes, turreted castles, Milan cathedrals, Spanish Alhambras, all breaking into each other with a bewitching haphazardness. Imagine the color of each a deep, cerulean blue, intensely so in the interior and paling towards the outward edges, and over this azure, silken sheen, a white lace veil, spider-wrought in its delicacy, thrown like a snowy cover. Imagine the light of the sun upon it, and a thousand tints and glints and shadows that transform and glorify the whole into a shimmering hill-chain of fire-hearted opals. Imagine a dying glacier to the left which looks like a mighty river caught in its downward career, and held cold and stiff in the hand of death. Imagine ice fields beyond, stretching back into the interior over thirty miles, further than the eye can reach, grim and awful in their calmness. Imagine mountains on all sides rearing their shining crests 6,000 feet in air. Imagine Glacier Bay at their feet clothed in silvery mist, on whose surface float sky-hued icebergs. Imagine brooding over all a deep silence, restful and unbroken as that in the heavenly spheres. Imagine all this, and you have the Muir as it stands to-day.

On the day of our arrival in Sitka the Hon. John G. Brady received his " credentials " ratifying his appointment by President McKinley as governor of the vast territory of Alaska.

Before making the journey to Alaska Mrs. Brady had written that she would be my hostess while I was in Sitka. As soon as the steamer anchored an old Indian guide was employed to conduct me to the home of Mrs. Brady. After passing through several streets of the queer little town, and along the water-front of a dirty Indian village, we reached a modern residence which my heretofore silent companion indicated by certain grunts and signs to be my destination. Mrs. Brady greeted me cordially. On learning that my stay in Sitka would be but for a few hours, she suggested that we go from house to house, to tell the people of my mission in order to secure an audience, and hold a meeting that evening.

Acting upon her suggestion, we went from one end

of the town to the other,—to the newspaper office, the home of the Episcopal bishop, the Presbyterian mission, the dwellings of the Russians, everywhere, explaining the work of the Woman's Christian Temperance Union and urging attendance at the evening service. At nine o'clock, while light was still in the heavens, we went to the little Presbyterian church and I spoke to the people assembled and organized a W. C. T. U.— almost under the pole-star. That night Governor and Mrs. Brady accompanied me to the *Queen*, and early next morning the ship moved away from Sitka.

On returning to Tacoma we found the city in a blaze of excitement over the discovery of the Klondike gold fields, whose fabulous riches have since lured so many to fortune or to doom.

My travels and lecture work continued through eastern Oregon and Washington, Idaho, Montana, Wyoming, Utah and Colorado. I rested from my labors for several days in Yellowstone Park, whose wonders would fill a volume, then continued farther westward, stopping en route in Nevada and again spending some time in Southern California and, on my way home, speaking in Arizona, Texas, New Mexico and Louisiana.

CHAPTER XXIV

" THE LATTER DAY SAINTS "

The people of the United States are more sensible of the disgrace of Mormonism than of its danger. The civilized world wonders that such a hideous caricature of the Christian religion should have appeared in this most enlightened land.— JOSIAH STRONG.

THERE is no place in the Union as unique in every particular as Salt Lake City. It is made so by a peculiar people—the Mormons—whose strange religious faith sets them apart from all the rest of the world. Driven from the states on account of their repugnant doctrines, they found a refuge in the desert of Utah, which they have transformed into a modern garden of Hesperides. The city sits at the base of the Wasatch Mountains, the breath from whose cool summits invigorates and strengthens. The streets are very broad and smooth, shaded by numerous trees and rendered attractive by handsome homes and business blocks. Temple Square is the centre of religious life, and the leading object of the admiration of both Mormon and Gentile. Here are found three magnificent structures. First and always the Temple, that wonder of architectural beauty and splendor. It was made of pure white granite taken from a cañon in Utah. It was forty years in process of erection, and cost almost $6,000.000. With the exception of the Roman Catholic cathedral in New York, it is the most superb house of worship in America. The Tabernacle is a mammoth building almost circular in shape, and having the appearance of a gigantic turtle upon the outer side. Its utmost seating capacity is said to be eleven thousand, the great gallery holding nearly as many as the main floor. The wood-work of the superb organ came from the forests of Utah. The choir, composed of five-hundred voices, is wholly voluntary. The acoustic properties of the building are exceedingly rare.

While in Salt Lake City I addressed an audience in the Tabernacle. One of the wives of Brigham Young, a Mormon woman doctor, some members of the W. C. T. U. and several officials of the Mormon church occupied seats on the terraced platform. B. H. Roberts, the polygamous Mormon, whose admission to Congress was refused, offered prayer, and other ecclesiastics performed different rôles. It was a strange and interesting experience.

The Assembly Hall is an elegant building, like an opera house upon the inner side. These three structures are within one enclosure; a huge wall shuts them out from the busy street, and around the Temple is a strong iron fence, beyond which the foot of a Gentile is not allowed to enter. None but the saints go into the sacred precincts. * During the years that the Temple was being built the priests, in order to keep up the courage of the Mormons and stimulate them to greater zeal and

* The facts stated in this chapter were obtained from leading Gentiles and Mormons in Salt Lake City.

activity in raising money for its completion, told them
that as soon as the Temple was finished the Lord would
come and occupy a room in it. When the last touches
had been given, and the Temple stood an assured real-
ity, and the Lord did not come, Elder Woodruff, president of the State Church, said he had a revelation from
God that He was offended because the Gentiles had been
allowed to gain a foothold in Utah, and that Christ
would not appear. Further, that the wrath of God
could be appeased only by unceasing work to evangelize
the world. They are now sending out their missionaries by the hundreds; some of them boys not out of
their teens. By this means, and the thorough organization of the church in every branch, Mormonism is
growing tremendously. It cannot be realized or ap-
preciated by those who are far removed from its centre,
or who have never been given an object-lesson of its
strength.

While I was in Salt Lake City the Annual Conference
of the Mormons was held. Men and women poured
into the Tabernacle day after day from the most remote
corners of Utah and adjoining states. Some conception
of the vastness of the movement was gained when I saw
that great auditorium packed from door to door at a
morning business session. Imagine what it would be at
an evening meeting. At this conference the elders and
bishops and other high church dignitaries occupied the
three rows of seats that stand one above the other in a
semi-circle facing the main body of the edifice. Without introduction one man after another arose and addressed the people. At the close of each harangue the

speaker said: " In the name of Jesus Christ, amen! " and all the audience answered, " Amen." During this especial conference the burden of each orator's effort was to inveigh against the priesthood being criticized by the church members. " When that begins," said one mighty in authority, " then comes darkness and death to Mormonism." Their leading thought, however, was that the revelations of God to a people must be given by human agencies; and, secondly, these agencies must be beyond all cavil. Elder Merrill said, " The Bible is good, and the Book of Mormon is good, but give me the living oracles of the church." Apostle Taylor then took up the song, beginning with Noah and going on down to Joseph Smith, to prove that the written Word was insufficient through which God could reveal himself to the world. " Other churches have the Word given by men; ours is given by direct revelation. Joseph Smith had this revelation, and it has been given to us ever since! " cried one of the enthusiasts.

The Mormon church is supported by tithes, each man and woman contributing a certain portion of their income or earnings, and the church has become very rich through it. Another mode of increasing the treasury is by baptisms for the dead. There are priests who are always officiating in the Temple, and thousands of baptisms are performed every day. Some persons are baptized hundreds of times. At each baptism a sum of money is paid for the ceremony, and the issuance, by degrees, of the tormented soul from hell assured.

The Mormons are devoted pleasure-loving people, and all their pursuits in that line are sanctioned by the church. Their dances are always opened with prayer, the bishop usually officiating on the occasion. The church and state are closely united in Mormonism. No man runs for a political office who is in any way connected with the machinery of the church, unless the church approves. In Salt Lake City the functionaries of Mormonism have their offices in a large building in the business section of the town, and here, too, are found the tithe-houses. For years the Mormons were not regarded as Christians by the outside world. They speak of this bitterly. Christ is recognized prominently in their worship, but usually upon the same basis as Joseph Smith. The following incident will explain volumes. A little Mormon girl, returning from Sunday-school one Sabbath day, was accosted by a Gentile lady, and the ensuing conversation occurred: " Do you like to go to Sunday-school, dearie? "

" Yes, ma'am."

" What have you been studying lately? "

" I have just been learning about Moses and Jesus Christ. Now we are going to study about Joseph Smith."

The whole structure of Mormonism was conceived of and carried into execution by shrewd, cunning men. Joseph Smith is canonized among the Mormons, and his fame sounded through successive generations as a prophet from God. Brigham Young's statue occupies a conspicuous position in the leading street of Salt Lake City, and his praises are sung by the Latter Day Saints. His process of hoodwinking is gigantic. At one time, it is said, he issued a manifesto that he had received a revelation from God to the effect that only a certain sort of tree should be planted by the Mormons in Utah, and he had these trees in his nursery. At once all the faithful cut down their trees and ordered others from President Young. When the new trees were three years old he had another revelation that God was again displeased with the variety, and desired a different kind. Once more the trees were all cut down, and a sort entirely unlike the others ordered from Brigham Young's nursery. This occurred three times, the orders all being filled from the same source. He reaped a goodly harvest from the credulity of the people. A second story similar to this is told of the president. When the saints had accumulated thousands of heads of hogs, Brigham Young said it was declared to him in a revelation from God that no swine should be used by the Mormons; but Brigham, in the generosity of his soul, sorry to have his brethren suffer the loss, bought up all the hogs and sold them at a fabulous price to the emigrants passing through Utah on their way to the far West. In addition to all these statesman-like manœuvers, Brigham Young added to his wealth by seven breweries.

When the law was enforced abolishing polygamy there were 1500 Mormons in jail at one time in Salt Lake City, both men and women. If a child were born in a polygamous marriage, but made its advent in another state, it and its parents were free if the infant was kept away from Utah for three years. This was called "outlawing a child." In the first stages of the Edmunds-Tucker enforcing act many hundreds of children were "outlawed," but since Utah has gained statehood polygamy is practised more openly by those who had contracted plural marriages in the earlier years of the movement.

It had been the wonder of my life how any woman could enter a polygamous marriage. When I arrived in Salt Lake City and met some of the leading women of the church of the Latter Day Saints and talked with them about their religion and home affairs, I realized the motive power that had induced them to be wedded to men who either had other wives or would take unto themselves others. The majority of the women of the older set were converted to Mormonism in their early years. Marriage and motherhood were held up as requisites by which to attain unto eternal life, and the greater sacrifices a woman makes in these lines the greater will be her exaltation after death.

They entered polygamy from an intense religious enthusiasm, actuated by the same promptings that lead a nun into the convent or a martyr to the stake. This principle is still alive in the hearts of the more conscientious Mormon women; but as the years have gone by and the power of the church increased, of course there have been thousands of women who entered polygamous marriages from baser motives. I expected to find a dull, groveling lot of people in whom the animal was ever to the front. My amazement was unbounded as woman after woman was introduced who was the very acme of refinement, intelligence and often of beauty.

One of the foremost leaders of thought among the Mormon women edits a paper in Salt Lake City and is a devoted club woman. She has represented the women of Utah in the National Council of Women and appeared before congressional committees to secure measures for the advancement of her people. She was educated in Massachusetts, and when in her teens she accepted the Mormon faith and crossed the plains with other pioneers in the days of the noted exodus. Like any other business personage, she has her office in the city and is as full of affairs as the most energetic man in the blocks about her.

At a reception given to me by Mormon women in a Mormon woman's home in Salt Lake City, I met typical Mormon women of every degree. The house in which the reception was held is an elegant structure with stained glass windows and rich furniture; every curtain and carpet and picture in exquisite harmony. The hostess was a woman of wide culture; she had traveled extensively in this country and abroad and was the very essence of high-bred grace and polished manner. Her five daughters, dressed in perfect taste, and having inherited their mother's gentleness and attractiveness, helped to do the honors of the occasion most beautifully. On leaving the reception, I said to a Mormon woman who accompanied me:

" You don't mean to tell me that our hostess is one of many wives of some man, do you? "

" Oh, yes! " was the quick, cheerful reply. " She is the second wife. The first lives not far from her on an adjoining street."

Among other noted Mormon women in Salt Lake City, are Dr. Martha Hughes Cannon, who was elected

to the Senate of Utah, a practising physician, and Mrs.
Zina D. Young, one of the nineteen wives of Brigham
Young. The latter is a vivacious old lady, near three
score and ten years of age. She is called " aunt Zinie "
—" aunt " being a title of love and respect among
the Latter Day Saints, just the same as that we honor
the older negro women in the South. In the home
of Mrs. Zina D. Young I was shown the celebrated
painting of " Joseph, the Prophet," which hangs in a
room filled with portraits of Brigham Young and other
apostles and evangelists of the Mormon church. The
home of " aunt Zinie " is an unpretentious cottage sit-
uated on a quiet street.

Prominent objects of Salt Lake City, scarcely second
in interest to the Temple and Tabernacle, are the dwellings of Brigham Young called " Bee-hive " and " Lion-
House," where he kept his many wives, and the palace
of Amelia, his favorite wife, that stands on the opposite
side of the street. The latter has been confiscated since
the abolition of polygamy, and " Bee-hive " and " Lion-
House " have also passed into other hands, but it is
understood that the wives who are still living are well
provided for, as President Brigham Young left a large
fortune. The younger Mormon men and women do not
usually enter into polygamous marriages, but, it is said,
on incontrovertible authority, that polygamy is still
practised by the older people who had contracted plural
marriages before the Edmunds-Tucker law went into
effect. Numbers of Mormon women are rearing large
families of children without any visible husbands, not
only in Salt Lake City but in states adjoining Utah; and

these women are held in high repute among the Mormons, thus showing that they are regarded as legally wedded.

When I was going to Salt Lake City the train stopped at a wayside station for supper. A pretty girl about thirteen years of age was selling glasses of milk from a large tin bucket that she carried on her arm. She had a winsome face and I asked: " Are you a little Mormon girl?" " Yes," was the demure reply. " Have you many brothers and sisters?" " Quite a number." " How many wives has your father?" " Two." " Does he live with both?" " Yes." " Which is your mother?" " The first." " Do you like the other?" " Yes, of course! why shouldn't I?" she demanded with blazing eyes, and with a disdainful snap of her bucket-top she marched off. Poor little thing! She had the fire and loyalty of the usual Mormon woman, and of every other woman who believes in a cause whether right or wrong and has to suffer for it.

The wonder and glory of Utah is Great Salt Lake. This marvel in nature " covers an area of 2300 square miles." Its depth is seldom greater than twenty feet, but at the deepest point it is sixty feet. Its waters are as clear as crystal, and the sand at the bottom, which is plainly seen, is a grayish white. There are several islands in Great Salt Lake, and the mountains are round about it. A storm upon it, or a sunset, is a sight calculated to fill one with awe and admiration. At a point upon the outer edges, where the desert joins the lake, the waters have been gradually cut off; the dry air quickly evaporates the moisture, leaving shining beds of salt glistening in the light. Heavy rollers drawn by horses are passed over these; then the crystalline mass is shoveled up, put into sacks, and placed on the cars, which run close to the fields of salt, and shipped to the outside world.

Saltair is the name of a mammoth bath-house built out in the waters of Salt Lake. To this huge pavilion thousands resort every summer to enjoy the exhilarating effects of a float on Salt Lake. " Going down into the water " here can hardly be called a bath, as the water is so densely impregnated with salt that one's body is borne up lightly like a cork; and if the head and feet are not submerged, can glide over the face of the sea like a fleck of down. The finest saloon in Utah is at Saltair. It is run by leading Mormons. Up to twenty-eight years ago the Latter Day Saints were undisturbed in their desert retreat, but since the mining interests have grown so important in Utah, the state has become settled by hordes of Gentiles until now, really, the population and appearance of the country is very much like other localities, except that, underneath the surface, the Mormons still have their hold upon material prosperity and religious power.

CHAPTER XXV

For looking backward through the year,
  Along the path my feet have pressed,
I see sweet places everywhere,—
  Sweet places where my soul had rest.
                              —PHOEBE CARY.

WHILE in Salt Lake City I spoke at several meetings held in the interest of the temperance cause and lectured once on Alaska. The state convention of the Woman's Christian Temperance Union was in session a part of the time. Some of the greatest audiences that it has been my pleasure to address, greeted me in the West. Those in certain portions of California, Utah, and Colorado being particularly gratifying. One of the most interesting places which I visited in Colorado was Cripple Creek, the famous mining camp. The whole country in the gold belt surrounding the place presents a most novel and engaging appearance to a stranger. Numberless prospects cover the face of the hills. A " prospect " is a venture at mining, looking for paying ore. If not found in sufficient quantities to meet and go above all expense of operation, the venture remains forever a prospect. If the precious metals in paying quantities are found, it is called a " mine." The population of the mining district of Cripple Creek was at that time estimated at 40,000. In the town itself it had reached the large number of 20,000. It is wonderful how human beings flock to these rich mining camps; how they suffer privations and work like galley-slaves for gold. I found educated men at Cripple Creek delving in the mines, while their wives cooked and did every kind of hard work, living in two-room huts in the back yards of persons who were equally cramped and equally hard-worked. The open saloons, gambling dens and dance-houses flourish with a brazen effrontery not seen in older haunts of civilization. At the "Branch," the Monte Carlo of Cripple Creek, gambling is carried on with a high hand. The rooms are magnificently furnished; soft velvet carpets cover the floors, and elegant oil paintings of the most immoral subjects decorate the walls. Here the men flock to scatter their hard-earned dollars at faro, poker, etc., while the "Branch" proprietor, loaded with diamonds, looks on complacently. In this institution there is a palace saloon in which there is a bar of heavily carved oak with beaten brass ornamentations, costing nothing less than $20,000. In other drinking establishments similar furnishings are found, and musicians are stationed near the door to beguile the wayfarer into their depths by bewitching strains of exquisite melody. The miners go to the "Branch" to get their checks cashed. In one day the amounts rise as high as $12,600. Vice of a lower order than drinking and gambling stalks unrebuked through the streets of Cripple Creek, in the glare of daylight as well as in the shades of night.

On my arrival at the mining camp an afternoon meeting was held with some W. C. T. U. women. It was said that all the churches in the place were either too small to accommodate the desired audience or were occupied with protracted services; so in order to reach the crowd the alternative was to go on the streets at night, and to talk in the open air. That evening at 8 o'clock, accompanied by the president of the local society, I stood on the corner of a crowded thoroughfare and spoke to hundreds of people thronging the way.

At the close of the meeting, reinforced by another friend, we visited the saloons, the dance-halls and the most prominent gambling dens. In the rear of one of the grog-shops were found two young men, one frail and pallid, seated at a piano; the other leaning against a whiskey barrel. They were both singing a pathetic melody, the chorus ending with, " I am an outcast, a wanderer; I am far from home to-night." We stopped to listen. Going over the words a second time the boy-pianist looked at us unsmilingly and said, " That means me! " As we walked down the sin-cursed street, for blocks the plaintive refrain followed us on the summer air, " I am an outcast, a wanderer." Doubtless hundreds of hearts in Cripple Creek responded to the plaint. A short distance beyond Colorado Springs, is found South Cheyenne Cañon, noted for its wonderful scenery and as the place where Helen Hunt Jackson desired her body to be buried. The cañon is short, but stupendous. Ponderous granite mountains come so near together that on first sight it seems impossible that a roadway could ever be forged between them. It looks as if a mighty hand had pried the boulders apart, and that they may at any time close up their ranks again. In the grandest part of the cañon are found Seven Falls that present a scene full of entrancing loveliness. The granite has been smoothly terraced by mother nature in seven different places in a great gorge, and over these surge volumes of water clear as crystal. At this point the carriage is abandoned and, climbing up several flights of steps hundreds of feet high, the brow of a mountain is gained and at once commences a search for the sacred spot where the body of that sweet singer and romance writer, Helen Hunt Jackson, was laid to rest. It is found on the slope overlooking the yawning clefts in the cañon and in close proximity to the Seven Falls, —a cool, peaceful nook under the sighing pines. A mass of stones now lie on the empty grave, and between these are wedged numerous cards of visitors who desired to let the hawks and eagles and mountain-grasses know that their majesties had called.

Helen Hunt Jackson died in San Francisco. In her last days she requested that she be buried in South Cheyenne Cañon. As soon as was practicable, her husband had her body brought from the city, where it was laid temporarily, and carried over the mountain heights by a carriage-road to her favorite place, where she had often sat and read and written far removed from the din and strife of the outside world. Only a few friends formed the mournful party as it filed its way through the mountain fastnesses with its precious burden to the abiding place that had been chosen above all on earth

in which to wait for the resurrection morn. The burial-
ground was so unusual that it attracted hordes of visitors, who began to make it a rendezvous for picnics and
headquarters for advertisements. The notoriety and
accompanying desecration grew so offensive to Mr.
Jackson that he had his wife's remains removed to the
cemetery at Colorado Springs, and the grave marked by
a modest headstone. Helen Hunt Jackson will linger
forever in the memory of mankind as the friend of the
Indian,—" Romona " and " A Century of Dishonor "
immortalizing her as the strongest advocate for that unfortunate race known in the literary or philanthropic
world.

After the long absence of almost nine months, during which I traveled thousands of miles and had numberless strange experiences, going back to my blessed
old plantation home was looked forward to with greater
eagerness than in all my life before, especially as I came
with health fully restored. A hearty welcome awaited
me as always from mother and father, who were ever
in such perfect accord and sympathy with my public
work. Oh! the joy, the abandon, the peace, the inde-
scribable sweetness in one's *own* home such as is found
nowhere else on earth!

At mine there is rest of body and *soul* for
me. Everything is kept quiet. Mother's solicitude
goes so far as to prompt her to station little
negroes at strategic points about the yard to prevent the roosters from coming within hearing distance of my windows, fearing their crowing may
disturb me. In the afternoons, when my usual walk is

taken over the hills and through the beautiful woods, a
delegation of eight or twelve young black boys and girls
accompanies me. They usually return laden with flowers
and grasses and always expect remuneration of some
sort; so I have them stand in line and rejoice their
hearts by filling their hands with sugar. Off they
scamper,—eating as they go. At Christmas, the custom
of all the negroes on the plantation is to rush into the
" white folks' " house one by one or in groups and cry,
" Chris'mus giff! I done cotch you fust. " Every one
expects a present of some sort, if nothing more than a
bit of fruit or a stick of candy; but there *must* be *something,* in order to prevent the deepest disappointment.
In ante-bellum days each was remembered generously;
every old ex-slave still expects it and they have handed
down this expectation to their descendants.

Just after supper, in the spring and summer, father
and I sit on the front gallery and talk as freely and con-
fidentially as in my young girlhood. In winter, after
the evening meal, mother reads to me for two hours.
On these visits home, I hug the fleeting hours to my
soul; so full are they of happiness and satisfaction. The
pain of parting from my dear ones has never grown less
poignant. While life lasts I cannot forget the picture
which is repeated at each of my departures. The waiting vehicle at the front gate, the horse held by some old
negro servant. Father suffering visibly, but smiling
bravely, saying, " God bless you, daughter, and bring
you back in safety to us." Mother folding me to her
heart and sobbing, " Good-bye, darling! Good-bye, my
precious one." My youngest brother walking briskly

up and exclaiming, "Do come on, sister! You will never catch the train in time." As we drive under the cedars, on looking back, father is seen busily engaged examining the fixtures of the gate and mother is walking back and forth on the long gallery, crying, " Goodbye, darling, good-bye!" And yet, they would not have me leave the work and remain with them for all the gold in Alaskan hills.

CHAPTER XXVI

THE OLD PLANTATION HOME

Should auld acquaintance be forgot,
And never brought to mind,
Should auld acquaintance be forgot,
And days of auld lang syne.

FOR several weeks during the winter of 1897-98 Miss
Jessie Ackerman was my guest at the plantation. She
was very much interested in the colored people and requested the privilege of holding a meeting with some
of them in our dining-room and of furnishing the refreshments. She desired to invite only fifty and these
to be limited to the ex-slaves of the Kearney family.
New Year's day was appointed for the gathering.
Long before the noon hour our dusky guests began to
arrive. Some came in respectable buggies driving well-
groomed horses, some in lumbering farm wagons;
others rode mules or walked. They were comfortably
clothed and ragged, middle-aged and old, strong and
feeble. One stumped in on a peg leg, his original member having been torn off in a cotton-gin " since de
wah; " rheumatism had sentenced another to crutches,
and one came with tightly bandaged head to cover an
empty eye socket; but all felt very high-toned and important and representative of the family dignity. The

dining-room had been decked and garnished for many hours in anticipation of the unusual event. There were great branches of holly, rich in its dark green leaves and crimson berries, graceful, grey sprays of trailing Spanish moss, and clusters of mistletoe banked over the mantel, the pictures, the sideboard, the window-frames, —at every point of vantage. In the centre of the large table a huge basket of fruit peeped out from between drooping vines, and cakes and nuts and candies completed an artistic and enticing decoration.

The negroes stood in solid ranks about the table. Father had declined to act as master of ceremonies, as he was not well, and mother also refused the honor, which consequently devolved upon me. Near the door leading into the hall father stood, looking very worn and feeble, near him were my youngest brother and guests who had dined with us; further on Miss Ackerman and myself, and beyond us sat mother.

I opened the ceremonies by announcing that the agreeable occasion had been planned and carried out by Miss Ackerman; that she had furnished the good things and wanted them all to have a happy time. After telling them of her travels and work as a missionary, Miss Ackerman was introduced. She fired their enthusiasm by a stirring speech. When she related the incident of walking on the bottom of the ocean, of lying in the ear of a god in India, and portrayed the terrors of a storm at sea, they gave a long, low, whining groan and pressed nearer together, swaying to and fro. At the close of her address the meeting was thrown open and different persons

were called upon for testimonies. We thought to make
it a love-feast and to be edified by many ripe Christian
experiences; but it took a different turn. " Aunt Miry,"
an old woman on crutches, who was one of grandmother's house servants, was the first one asked to
speak. Without hesitating a moment she said: " Whoever would er thought that I could er cum inter Marse
Walter's house lak dis! It makes me think might'ly o'
de time when ole mis' wur er livin', " then there followed a short dissertation, in mournful intonations, on
the good old times when she " had ben tuk kyar uv an'
everybody had plenty and to spar'."

Numbers of men and women followed in the note
struck by " Aunt Miry." The pathos deepened; mother
left the room. Father was the " Marse Walter " referred to in the speeches. I watched his face as the
meeting progressed. His eyes filled slowly with tears
and his lips trembled with suppressed emotion. Finally
" Uncle Jim Fisher " was called on; he had been one of
grandfather's slaves and was the old man with the
empty eye-socket, left so by an invading sliver of iron
while he worked in a blacksmith shop. Lifting his sad
face reverentially he said in measured tones as if chant-
ing a requiem: " Holy, holy, holy! O, how sweet to be
in my young Marster's house dis day! *Look* at my
young Marster! fresh an' fine, jes' off de vine! " pointing to father, aged and feeble, but who was never
anything but beautiful in the eyes of the old slave who
remembered him only and always as the handsome
" young **marster**" of brilliant youth.

Uncle Jim's speech was the most grandiloquent of

the day, and the most touching. When he finished father's indisposition was forgotten. His soul was awake and his mind stirred with memories of a hallowed past; especially with the part he had played in the great drama so intimately allied with the destiny of the race whose representatives now before him had been held in slavery by himself and his kinsmen. Stepping quietly to the front he threw back his head, assuming an attitude peculiar to him when deeply moved, and made a strong, tender speech to those dark friends of happier days. Pressing about him closely they began to moan, crying softly with uplifted faces bathed in tears. "I have been your friend and shall be unto the end," were father's closing words. "Dat's so! Marse Walter, dat's so!" "Praise Gord, dat *sho* is so!" came from all parts of the room.

Finally, Harrison Green, the only preacher present, was asked to pray. He was a Hercules in ebony—one of mother's former slaves. Closing his eyes and stiffening his neck he made a prayer distinctive of the negro pastor in his unlettered, unfettered religious frenzy,— abjectly heart-revealing, boisterously sin-denunciatory, crowded with heaven ascending ejaculations and hell descending imprecations, all punctured with stentorian groans that appalled the ear and dismayed the soul. Miss Ackerman had provided fifty paper bags to be filled with the refreshments and taken home by her colored guests. When everybody had been served, Harrison Green, the inflated preacher, said to me, "Miss Belle, yer mus' call dis yer meetin' ter order agin an' give me er chance ter say er word to dese yer folks."

Silence was restored. Walking ostentatiously to a small
table near, pushing his hands into his pockets and scru-
tinizing the faces of his hearers, Harrison said: " Look
here, niggers! is yer gwine ter brek up dis here meetin'
in er onmannerly fashion, an' let dis strange white
'ooman leave widout returnin' her sum perliteness by
depressin' our thanks?" Wheeling around to Miss
Ackerman, he continued: " We is pow'ful' bleeged ter
yo', my sister, for dese yer things yer gin us fer ter
eat, but pow'fuller more thankful for what yer tole us
in yo' speech. Before yo' go away, 'dough, I think
yo' had better tell us how to raise our chilluns." Shak-
ing his fist in sudden wrath at the group of boys and
girls on the opposite side of the room who had crept in
unnoticed and who were now chattering like guineas
and cracking nuts with their shining teeth, he exclaimed: " Shut up dat fuss, niggers! Ain' yer got no
manners 'fore white folks?" Cooling down again and
altering his voice to the ministerial tone, one hand thrust
out in mild gesticulation, he said to his colored friends:
" Now my bredderin, a partin' an' a farewell word ter
yo' an' me is dis: we mus' be so ongrateful fer what dis
here strange white 'ooman has done fer us dis New
Year Day as to make us more inconsistent accordin'
ter our religious departments fru all de years what am
ter cum."

After the benediction was pronounced " de meetin'
broke up." Then the women came in a shy way to greet
Miss Ackerman and me. What they said to her she did
not tell, but one old woman, holding my hand in both
her horny ones said: " Honey, doan' yer know *me?* My

gal, Jemimy Jane, she *nussed* yer." Another, after a hearty handshake, exclaimed: "Lor', little missy! I ain' seen yer since yer wur er chile. My gal, Drunella Clarissy, *nussed* yer!" In mother's room I heard Sally, the heroine of the silver and Federal soldiers, saying: "Humph! Dat white lady *may* be er traveler but she cyant tell me much. I'se seed storms on de Gulf o' Mexico when I use ter go down dar wid mistis' jes' 'bout as big as her in ennybody else has ever saw. Gwine down inter de bottom o' de ocean an' layin' in de year o' dat gord I doan' know nuthin' 'bout. I *sho* ain' done *dat!* But I jes' knows one thing: what dis here nigger an' her white folks has seed am *sholy* hard to beat!"

CHAPTER XXVII

THE LAST FAREWELL

Thank God that, looking across a grave,
The world's dim vision clears,
Till Calvary lies in the golden glow
Of God's eternal years.— MARY T. LATHRAP.

EIGHTEEN HUNDRED NINETY-EIGHT was another
fateful year to me. In January a business trip
was made to Jackson, Mississippi. In the early
dawn of a cold, grey morning I was seated in a
train for the purpose of returning home. The only person in the car besides myself was a lady who sat at some
distance behind me. In a few moments a gentleman,
very Western and very noticeable in appearance, entered. Approaching me he lifted his hat and said
hesitatingly, "Excuse me, but I followed you because
I thought I knew you." There was a quizzical look on
his face which I construed as amusement. Thinking
that the stranger's purpose in accosting me was simply
to form an acquaintanceship to relieve the *ennui* of
travel, all my Puritanical instincts rebelled. With a
repellant air I said, "Yes?" Considerably disconcerted
but evidently intent on discovering my identity he scru-
tinized my hand satchel for a name, and with a search-

ing gaze into my eyes asked: "Is this Miss Belle Kearney?" "It is, sir," was my reply, stiffer than before. A radiant smile passed over the gentleman's face and bending toward me he said in low, sweet tones that began to sound wonderfully familiar, "Have the years washed out *all* remembrance? I am your brother!"

It required then only a moment to recognize the beloved comrade of early days, who read Shakspeare with me and helped to build the " castles in the air." There was the same tall, lithe figure, but with a man's sinewy strength and graceful dignity in place of the boyish bearing that filled my memory. Since leaving Mississippi for the West, at seventeen years of age, he had lived in Texas, Mexico and the mountains of New Mexico. In all that time he had returned home but. once.

After three days only, spent together on the plantation, I was forced to leave to fill some lecture engagements. My brother had never heard me speak, so he accompanied me to my next two appointments. On the last day we dined together at a dear friend's home. In the afternoon I stood on the front porch and waving my hand to him called out: "Farewell, dear heart! Come home to us every year after this, won't you?" A smiling good-bye was answered and he was gone. Little did I dream then that we should never meet again on earth.

> "Was it so long? It seems so brief a .while
>   Since this still hour between the day and dark
> Was lightened by a little fellow's smile;
>   Since we were wont to mark

The sunset's crimson dim to gold, to gray,
    Content to know that, though he loved to roam
Care-free among the comrades of his play,
    Twilight would lead him home.

" But if we so, with eager eyes and glad,
    Looked forward to his coming in the gloom;
If so our hearts leaped out to meet the lad
    Whose smiles lit all the room—
Shall there not be a Presence waiting thus
    To still the bitter craving of the quest?
Shall there not be a welcome, too, for us
    When we go home to rest? "

The following summer my headquarters were made
at a quiet little village on Narragansett Bay. I was the
guest of my beloved friends, Ednah B. Hale and E.
Carol Hodge, who are the gifts of God to me. While
resting in their seaside cottage, the awful tidings
reached me of the sudden death of the noble brother
from whom I had so recently parted. Immediately after
his visit to us in the spring he went to Las Cruces, New
Mexico, where he intended to make his future home
engaging in the practice of law. My precious brother!
Out of the shadows of the earth-life he has stepped;
the sunlight is over there. Surely our Father has prepared for him a place where his God-given faculties can
find their full development, where he can grow into
" the perfect stature." Surely there awaited him the
unspeakable bestowment of immortality—a happy,
peaceful, glorified immortality. In the intuitive, divinely wrought assurance that had come to me, I asked
no questions of God. I was conscious of no rebellion.

I lifted my thoughts calmly to Him, and with eyes un-dimmed with tears and lips untrembling with sobs, I said: " It is all right, my Lord, whatever Thou sendest me. It is all right." This was the second brother who had gone out from us in less than three years; the first not quite thirty, this last nearly ending his thirty-first year.

Two scenes are stamped upon my brain and burned into my heart eternally. One October day in 1895—a little funeral procession moving slowly from the old home at Vernon across the sunlit fields. The open grave, the gleams of evening light and flickering shadows slanting across its sides and upon the coffin; the home-going, the fever, the semi-consciousness, the resting, the abiding, the all-rightness. In July, 1898, alien hands ministering to the young stranger hundreds of miles from home and loved ones, laid to rest at last by men whom the perils and the loneliness of the great American desert had made brotherly and loyal. Now there is a lonely grave at La Luz, in the far-away territory of New Mexico, in the depths of isolation, and the dreary winds, and the sweep and moan of the prairie grasses as they bend toward it—a lonely grave, and—God!

After it came—the message of death—I kept right on with my work. What else could I do? " For suffering and enduring there is no remedy but striving and doing." In the midst of the work and the loneliness,—the crowds and the stress of the human. Out of the darkness a voice was singing to my soul:

"The self-same twilight, cool, and calm, and dim,
  That led him home to us, despite our fears,
Shall lead us home to him!"

*　　*　　*　　*　　*

While on my way to New England in the summer of
1898, I stopped in Pulaski, Tennessee, to pay my respects to my venerable great-aunt, Mrs. Ann Lindsay,
who wore the crown of eighty-five years This gracious old lady discussed the Spanish war with absorbing
interest and showed me family relics more than a hundred years of age. At last she drew out the family
tree and began to descant upon it. She appeared to
conclude that so late born a " young American " needed
tutoring on ancestral lines. " My child," she said to
me, while her sixty-five-year-old bachelor-son stood by
and adjusted her white lace cap: " I suppose you know
that your great, great, great, great-grandfather was
Sir David, the Earl of Lindsay, of Scotland? and that
his son, James, came to America ' forward ' in the
seventeenth century, in the second or third fleet that
sailed into James river, and settled in Gloster county,
Virginia? and that your kinswoman, Mary Lindsay,
daughter of Joshua, son of James, son of Sir David,
married Edward Masterson, who was son of an Irish
earl? and that Ann Lindsay, daughter of John, son of
James, son of Joshua, son of old James the first, married
George Zollicoffer, son of John Jacob Zollicoffer, a
Swedish baron? and did you know that you are the
great, great, great, grand-daughter of Phillip Kearney
whose father was an Irish earl? And do you know that

the Lindsay coat-of-arms is Three Bullocks' Heads and the Bloody Yoke—livery blue, trimmed with red? You must apply to the Herald's office of the ancient government to get the Kearney and the Masterson coat-of-arms, not remembered by any present member of the family."

As the dear old lady talked on, the past now almost her only present, it was difficult to suppress a certain sense of the ludicrous. A scene of the long ago came before me; of my standing in the midst of my four brothers with this same family record in discussion, and of my saying, " Boys, when you marry I will frame a tree for each of you and present it on your wedding day." How they laughed, and one of them said derisively, " We had just as soon have so much sky! It isn't the family tree that counts *this* day in the world, but brains, brains, brains,—and the energy to back them! " It took me a long time to learn this wisdom, so early acquired by a boy's free contact with men; but after much sorrowful experience I did—thank God! Years of philanthropic work have taught me that " It's only noble to be good." However, I listened, interested, to my venerable aunt and later paid a visit with a heart full of reverence to a little grave-yard in the town of Pulaski, and searched out a long vault of stone under which lay the dust of one of my great, great-grandmothers. Upon the marble slab was written: " Sarah Kearney Lindsay, Died, 1774."

CHAPTER XXVIII

THE "HEAVENLY BIRTHDAY

A name earth wears forever next her heart;
One of the few that have a right to rank
With the true makers.—ANON.

THE month of February, 1898, found me in Washington City attending the annual convention of the National American Woman Suffrage Association. On entering the building where the sessions were being held on February seventeenth, a friend said to me: " Do you know Miss Willard is dead? She passed away this morning—just after midnight." On Saturday I was in New York city, where the funeral services were first to be held, accompanied by Mrs. S. D. La Fetra, former president of the W. C. T. U. of the District of Columbia. My desire was to see Anna Gordon at once. Our great leader had entered into everlasting life from the Empire Hotel. As soon as possible her remains had been carried to the home of her niece, Mrs. Katharine Willard Baldwin, at 85 Clinton Place.

About dusk, in the face of a driving wind and rainstorm, we found our way there. We were invited into a little sitting-room. The door opened gently, and Mrs. Baldwin entered. After a quiet, but cordial greeting, she began to tell us about the going of Miss Willard.

"Her death was very beautiful," she said; "much more beautiful than grandmother's, because she was younger. She looked like a little child—soft and sweet. At the last she was totally unconscious. The departure of her spirit was exceedingly peaceful. Her breath went out in three restful sobs, the last like a strain of music, the most exquisite I ever heard. She lies in there," pointing to an adjoining apartment. "Anna Gordon is to sleep in the room with her every night until she is taken away."

As we arose to leave, her eyes filled with tears, and she exclaimed: "I can't realize that Aunt Frank is dead! it seems so strange!" In the darkness we went to the Empire Hotel to see the W. C. T. U. women who were congregated there. It was a pathetic company of forlorn workers. As they sat or moved about, mournful and helpless, talking in low, awe-stricken tones of the one dearest in all the world to them, who had gone up higher, I thought of that little band of disciples in the long ago who stood desolate, gazing "steadfastly toward heaven" after their departing Lord, and the appearance of the angels in their midst. The Comforter was with us, too, that heart-breaking night, and the same sweet words came sifting into our souls: "Why stand ye gazing up into heaven? This same Jesus which is taken up from you into heaven shall so come in like manner as ye have seen him go into heaven;" and the blessed promise came with the thought: "Ye shall receive power after that the Holy Ghost is come upon you: and ye shall be witnesses unto me. . . to the uttermost part of the earth."

As the women talked the leading sentiment to which they gave expression was: " We have a common sorrow and a common joy. It is sweet for her to ' enter into rest,' but pitiful for us who stand in the shadow—waiting."

What pen of men or tongue of angels could summon words sufficiently strong or wise or tender in which to describe the work and the personality of this divinely inspired apostle of our Lord! Miss Willard's leadership was incomparable. She had the great power of drawing more people toward her, and of keeping them bound by the closest bonds of devotion, than any being that ever lived. The secret of it was that she was thoroughly true; true to herself, true to humanity, to which she gave her best; true to her heavenly calling and purpose, true to God. Miss Willard was a marvelous orator, organizer, author, statesman, Christian.

O, radiant spirit, O, sinless soul, thou hast won thy greatest victory! Thou hast conquered death and entered upon the eternal verities! Thou hast stood in the presence of the angels, and seen Christ face to face! " How beautiful it is to be with God."

For over nine years Miss Willard had been more to me than any woman who lived, except my mother. She was the leading inspiration of my life. She was never too busy to be loving, never too tired to be interested in those who followed the white ribbon banner, uplifted by her devoted hands. In all the care-filled days of her wonderful life she took time to send words of cheer and assurances of loyalty and appreciation for the smallest

thing done for Christ and humanity. On her way to
England she sent the following back to me,—only a
word of remembrance but invaluable as her words:

"U. S. M. S. ' NEW YORK '

Mar 12. 1895

Dearest Belle Kearney:

*I am moved
to write you a loving line.
Keep simple, humble,
devout; breathe in God;
study, increase. Go on.
— We have had a beautiful
voyage; all well; land this other
soon. Ever thy own Frances.*

On hearing of her death I felt that one of the foundations of my existence had slipped from under me and had drifted out to sea. Miss Willard was like no other human being. There was a divineness about her and a personal influence that no one else possessed. There will be many leaders, and great ones, but the world will never see just such a " chieftain " among women as Frances E. Willard. The great organization that grew to marvelous proportions under her matchless guidance has lost its ablest champion, the individuals who loved her their tenderest friend. After her death Lady Henry Somerset wrote in a personal letter, " It seems to me sometimes that the work that lies ahead and the loneliness of life are almost impossible to face; but the same Love that has cared for her and taken her to dwell in the Land where all is Love will encompass us and bring us at last to the haven where we would be, and where she is at rest." These heart testimonials have been written in the quietude of my old plantation home, in blessed communion with God and in sweet fellowship with mother and father, my best friends and loyal, loving comrades, standing now in the sunset glow of the evening of their lives:

" Only waiting till the shadows are a little longer grown," when their souls,

> " A glorious bridge will make
> Out of the golden bars,
> And all their precious treasures take
> Where shine the eternal stars."

With   the   dawn   of   the   untried   years   beaming

full upon me, through the swiftly opening gates of the twentieth century, here among the palm trees of Florida, its blossoms, its song-birds, its radiant sunshine, where my work has brought me in this year of grace, 1900, I consecrate myself anew to God, and cry as fervently as when the call of the Master first came to my life, over a decade ago, "Here am I, Lord. Send me!" give me strength of body and mind and spirit to work for the incoming of Thy Kingdom when not a being in all the world shall ask, through ignorance, "Who is Jesus of Nazareth?" when the gentleness of Christ shall supersede the inhumanity of man; when every institution is banished which causeth a tear or maketh a lie; when every law is so modified that no child shall cry for the loss of its birthright, nor a man mourn for his broken life, nor a woman weep for the possession of her heritage.

> "I know not what the future hath
>   Of marvel or surprise,
> Assured alone that life and death
>   His mercy underlies.

> "And so beside the Silent Sea
>   I wait the muffled oar;
> No harm from him can come to me
>   On ocean or on shore."

THE END.